Diesterwegs
Neusprachliche
Bibliothek

Sam Shepard

True West

With Additional Material

Edited and annotated
by
Albert-Reiner Glaap

VERLAG MORITZ DIESTERWEG
Frankfurt am Main

Abbreviations

e.g.	for example	*A.E.*	American English
i.e.	which is to say	s.o.	someone
cf.	compare	s.th.	something
pl.	plural	△	slang
fig.	figurative	●	colloquial
G.	German		

Die Szenenfotos zur Düsseldorfer Aufführung von *True West* stellte Frau Lore Bermbach zur Verfügung.

ISBN 3-425-04840-6

Satz: Karlheinz Stahringer, Ebsdorfergrund
Druck: graphoprint, Koblenz

Contents

Aspects of American English

Orthography mirrors pronunciation

a) Apostrophe at the beginnings of words

'at's	that's
'em	them
'course	of course
'fraid	afraid
'cause	because
'bout	about

b) Apostrophe at the end of words

a'	of
wanna'	want to
a lota'	a lot of
d'	do
gettin'	getting
somethin'	something
what sa'	what is the
whadya'	what do you
helluva'	hell of a
yer tryin'	you are trying
outa'	out of
shouldn't a'	shouldn't have
musta'	must have

c) Further Aspects

yeah	yes
nah	no
naw	no
ya	you
sorta	sort of
gonna	going to
kinda	kind of
I gotta	I have got to, I must
git	get
fer	for
forgit	forget
gimme	give me
jest	just
dunno	don't know
lemme	let me

Grammatical variants

she don't	she doesn't
don't it	doesn't it
he don't believe me	he doesn't believe me
that don't matter	that doesn't matter
I seen him	I saw him
he wouldn't a' gave	he wouldn't have given
I been tellin' you	I've been telling you
you shoulda' sen	you should have seen
you shouldn't oughta' take	you shouldn't take, you ought not to take
I didn't do nothin'	I didn't do anything

Characters

AUSTIN: Early thirties, light blue sports shirt, light tan cardigan sweater, clean blue jeans, white tennis shoes

LEE: His older brother, early forties, filthy white T-shirt, tattered brown overcoat covered with dust, dark blue baggy suit pants from the Salvation Army, pink suede belt, pointed black forties' dress-shoes scuffed up, holes in the soles, no socks, no hat, long pronounced sideburns, 'Gene Vincent' hairdo, two days' growth of beard, bad teeth

SAUL KIMMER: Late forties, Hollywood producer, pink and white flower-print sports shirt, white sports coat with matching polyester slacks, black and white loafers

MOM: Early sixties, mother of the brothers, small woman, conservative white skirt and matching jacket, red shoulder bag, two pieces of matching red luggage

The first performance of *True West* was given at The National Theatre on 23 November 1981 and was directed by John Schlesinger.

Set

All nine scences take place on the same set; a kitchen and adjoining alcove of an older home in a Southern California suburb, about forty miles east of L.A. The kitchen takes up the majority of the playing area to stage left (from the actor's point of view, facing the audience). The kitchen consists of a sink, up stage center, surrounded by counter space, a wall telephone, cupboards and a small window just above it bordered by neat yellow curtains. Stage left of sink

tan yellowish brown **cardigan sweater** woollen jacket that buttons up at the front **filthy** extremely dirty and unpleasant **tattered** old and torn **baggy** hanging in loose, untidy folds **pants** *A.E.* trousers **Salvation Army** *G.* Heilsarmee **suede** [sweɪd] *G.* Wildleder **dress-shoes** evening shoes **to scuff** to damage the shoe leather by walking carelessly etc. **sole** bottom of the shoe on which one walks **pronounced** very noticeable **sideburns** hair down the side on the face **Gene Vincent hairdo** the hairstyle of a famous American Rock-'n-Roll star at the beginning of the **1960**'s **slacks** loose-fitting trousers **loafers** *A.E.* a moccasin-like sports shoe
alcove ['ælkəʊv] a small, partly enclosed space in a room for a bed, bookshelves etc. **L.A.** Los Angeles **sink** *G.* Spülbecken **counter space** *G.* Arbeitsfläche

is a stove. Stage right, a refrigerator. The alcove adjoins the kitchen to stage right. There is no wall division or door to the alcove. It is open and easily accessible from the kitchen and defined only by the objects in it: a small, round, glass breakfast table mounted on white iron legs; two matching white iron chairs set across from each other. The two exterior walls of the alcove which prescribe a corner in the up stage right are composed of many small windows beginning from a solid wall about three feet high and extending to the ceiling. The windows look out to bushes and citrus trees. The alcove is filled with all sorts of house plants in various pots, mostly Boston ferns hanging in planters at different levels. The floor of the alcove is composed of green synthetic grass.

All entrances and exits are made stage left from the kitchen. There is no door. The actors simply go off and come onto the playing area.

Note on set and costume

The set should be constructed realistically with no attempt to distort its dimensions, shapes, objects or colors. No objects should be introduced which might draw special attention to themselves other than the props demanded by the script. If a stylistic "concept" is grafted onto the set design it will only serve to confuse the evolution of the characters' situation, which is the most important focus of the play.

Likewise, the costumes should be exactly representative of who the characters are, and not added onto for the sake of making a point to the audience.

Note on sound

The Coyote of Southern California has a distinct yapping, dog-like bark, similar to a Hyena. This yapping grows more intense and maniacal as the pack grows in numbers, which is usually the case when they lure and kill pets from suburban yards. The sense of growing frenzy in the pack should be felt in the background, particularly in Scenes Seven and Eight. In any case, these Coyotes never make the long, mournful, solitary howl of the Hollywood stereotype.

The sound of Crickets can speak for itself.

These sounds should also be treated realistically even though they sometimes grow in volume and numbers.

stove *G.* Küchenherd **accessible** easy to get into **to prescribe** to outline **planters** *A.E.* a decorative plant container **composed of** made of **to distort** to twist out of perspective **props** stage properties e.g. tables, chairs **script** the written form of a play or film **to graft onto** *G.* aufpfropfen **evolution** development **coyote** [kɔɪ'əʊt] *G.* Präriewolf, Kojote **yapping** short, sharp, excited barking **hyena** [haɪ'iːnə] *G.* Hyäne **maniacal** [mə'naɪəkl] *G.* manisch, besessen **pack** group of wild animals e.g. wolves **to lure** *G.* anlocken **frenzy** ['frenzɪ] state of wild, uncontrolled feeling **cricket** *G.* Grille

Act One

Scene One

Night, sound of crickets in dark, candlelight appears in alcove illuminating AUSTIN *seated at glass table, hunched over a writing notebook, pen in hand, cigarette burning in ashtray, cup of coffee, typewriter on table, stacks of paper, candle burning on table.*

Soft moonlight fills kitchen, illuminating LEE, *beer in hand, six pack on counter behind him, he's leaning against sink, mildly drunk, takes slug of beer.*

LEE: So, Mom took off for Alaska, huh?

AUSTIN: Yeah.

LEE: Sorta' left you in charge.

AUSTIN: Well, she knew I was coming down here so she offered me the place.

LEE: You keepin' the plants watered?

AUSTIN: Yeah.

LEE: Keepin' the sink clean? She don't like even a single tea leaf in the sink ya' know.

to hunch over to stand or bend over s.th. with rounded back **stack** untidy pile **slug** ● a single, big mouthful **to take off for** ● to leave **in charge** in control

AUSTIN: (*Trying to concentrate on writing*) Yeah, I know. (*Pause*)

LEE: She gonna' be up there a long time?

AUSTIN: I don't know.

LEE: Kinda' nice for you, huh? Whole place to yourself.

AUSTIN: Yeah, it's great.

LEE: Ya' got crickets anyway. Tons a' crickets out there. (*Looks around kitchen*). Ya' got groceries? Coffee?

AUSTIN: (*Looking up from writing*) What?

LEE: You got coffee?

AUSTIN: Yeah.

LEE: 'At's good. (*Short pause*). Real coffee? From the bean?

AUSTIN: Yeah. You want some?

LEE: Naw. I brought some uh—(*Motions to beer.*)

AUSTIN: Help yourself to whatever's—(*Motions to refrigerator.*)

LEE: I will. Don't worry about me. I'm not the one to worry about. I mean I can uh—(*Pause*) You always work by candlelight?

AUSTIN: No—uh—Not always.

LEE: Just sometimes?

AUSTIN: (*Puts pen down, rubs his eyes*) Yeah. Sometimes it's soothing.

LEE: Isn't that what the old guys did?

AUSTIN: What old guys?

LEE: The Forefathers. You know.

AUSTIN: Forefathers?

LEE: Isn't that what they did? Candlelight burning into the night? Cabins in the wilderness.

AUSTIN: (*Rubs hand through his hair*) I suppose.

LEE: I'm not botherin' you am I? I mean I don't wanna break into yer uh—concentration or nothin'.

AUSTIN: No, it's all right.

LEE: That's good. I mean I realize that yer line a' work demands a lota' concentration.

AUSTIN: It's okay.

LEE: You probably think that I'm not fully able to comprehend somethin' like that, huh?

AUSTIN: Like what?

LEE: That stuff yer doin'. That art. You know. Whatever you call it.

to motion to to point to **to soothe** [su:ð] to comfort, make calm **guys** *A.E.* men **forefathers** ancestors **to suppose** to think s.th. is right without knowing for certain **to bother s.o.** to disturb **to realize s.th.** to understand **stuff** ● work

AUSTIN: It's just a little research.

LEE: You may not know it but I did a little art myself once.

AUSTIN: You did?

LEE: Yeah! I did some a' that. I fooled around with it. No future in it.

AUSTIN: What'd you do?

LEE: Never mind what I did! Just never mind about that. (*Pause*) It was ahead of its time.

(*Pause*)

AUSTIN: So, you went out to see the old man, huh?

LEE: Yeah, I seen him.

AUSTIN: How's he doing?

LEE: Same. He's doin' just about the same.

AUSTIN: I was down there too, you know.

LEE: What d'ya' want, an award? You want some kinda' medal? You were down there. He told me all about you.

AUSTIN: What'd he say?

LEE: He told me. Don't worry.

(*Pause*)

AUSTIN: Well—

LEE: You don't have to say nothin'.

AUSTIN: I wasn't.

LEE: Yeah, you were gonna' make somethin' up. Somethin' brilliant.

(*Pause*)

AUSTIN: You going to be down here very long, Lee?

LEE: Might be. Depends on a few things.

AUSTIN: You got some friends down here?

LEE: (*Laughs*) I know a few people. Yeah.

AUSTIN: Well, you can stay here as long as I'm here.

LEE: I don't need your permission do I?

AUSTIN: No.

LEE: I mean she's my mother too, right?

AUSTIN: Right.

LEE: She might've just as easily asked me to take care of her place as you.

AUSTIN: That's right.

LEE: I mean I know how to water plants.

(*Long pause.*)

AUSTIN: So you don't know how long you'll be staying then?

to research to study a subject to find some new facts **never mind** it doesn't matter **award** prize **brilliant** amazingly intelligent **to depend on s.th.** *G.* von etwas abhängen **permission** agreement that s.o. may do s.th. **to take care of** to look after **place** home, house

LEE: Depends mostly on houses, ya' know.

AUSTIN: Houses?

LEE: Yeah. Houses. Electric devices. Stuff like that. I gotta' make a little tour first.

(*Short pause.*)

AUSTIN: Lee, why don't you just try another neighborhood, all right?

LEE: (*Laughs*) What'sa' matter with this neighborhood? This is a great neighborhood. Lush. Good class a' people. Not many dogs.

AUSTIN: Well, our uh—Our mother just happens to live here. That's all.

LEE: Nobody's gonna' know. All they know is somethin's missing. That's all. She'll never even hear about it. Nobody's gonna' know.

AUSTIN: You're going to get picked up if you start walking around here at night.

LEE: Me? I'm gonna, git picked up? What about you? You stick out like a sore thumb. Look at you. You think yer regular lookin'?

AUSTIN: I've got too much to deal with here to be worrying about—

LEE: Yer not gonna' have to worry about me! I've been doin' all right without you. I haven't been anywhere near you for five years! Now isn't that true?

AUSTIN: Yeah.

LEE: So you don't have to worry about me. I'm a free agent.

AUSTIN: All right.

LEE: Now all I wanna' do is borrow yer car.

AUSTIN: No!

LEE: Just fer a day. One day.

AUSTIN: No!

LEE: I won't take it outside a twenty-mile radius. I promise ya'. You can check the speedometer.

AUSTIN: You're not borrowing my car! That's all there is to it.

(*Pause*)

LEE: Then I'll just take the damn thing.

AUSTIN: Lee, look—I don't want any trouble, all right?

LEE: That's a dumb line. That is a dumb fuckin' line. You git paid fer dreamin' up a line like that?

AUSTIN: Look, I can give you some money if you need money.

devices equipment, products **lush** luxuriously comfortable **just happens** *G.* zufällig **to get picked up** ● to get arrested by the police **to stick out like a sore thumb** to seem very unsuitable and out of place **regular looking** ● *A.E. G.* anständig angezogen **to deal with** to occupy s.o. with, to keep s.o. busy **speedometer** [spɪˈdɒmɪtə(r)] instrument in a car which shows how fast one is travelling (= odometer) **damn** △ Kraftausdruck *G.* etwa: verdammt **that's a dumb line** ● that's a stupid thing to say

(LEE *suddenly lunges at* AUSTIN, *grabs him violently by the shirt, and shakes him with tremendous power.*)

LEE: Don't you say that to me! Don't you ever say that to me! (*Just as suddenly* LEE *turns* AUSTIN *loose, pushes him away and backs off.*) You may be able to git away with that with the old man. Git him tanked up for a week! Buy him off with yer Hollywood blood money, but not me! I can git my own money my own way. Big money!

AUSTIN: I was just making an offer.

LEE: Yeah, well keep it to yourself! (*Long pause.*) Those are the most monotonous fuckin' crickets I ever heard in my life.

AUSTIN: I kinda' like the sound.

LEE: Yeah. Supposed to be able to tell the temperature by the number a' pulses. You believe that?

AUSTIN: The temperature?

LEE: Yeah. The air. How hot it is.

AUSTIN: How do you do that?

LEE: I don't know. Some woman told me that. She was a Botanist. So I believed her.

AUSTIN: Where'd you meet her?

LEE: What?

AUSTIN: The woman Botanist?

LEE: I met her on the desert. I been spendin' a lota' time on the desert.

AUSTIN: What were you doing out there?

LEE: (*Pause, stares in space*) I forgit. Had me a Pit Bull there for a while but I lost him.

AUSTIN: Pit Bull?

LEE: Fightin' dog. Damn, I made some good money off that little dog. Real good money.

(*Pause*)

AUSTIN: You could come up north with me, you know.

LEE: What's up there?

AUSTIN: My family.

LEE: Oh, that's right, you got the wife and kiddies now don't ya'. The house, the car, the whole slam. That's right.

to lunge at to move forward suddenly e.g. with a sword **to grab** to take with a sudden, rough movement **violent** unusually strong and difficult to control **to shake** *G.* schütteln **tremendous** extreme **to get tanked up** ● to get drunk **to buy s.o. off** *G.* jdn. bestechen **offer** *G.* Angebot **fuckin'** △ Kraftausdruck *G.* Scheiß! **supposed to be able** they say you are able **desert** *G.* Wüste **Pit Bull (dog)** a particular kind of bulldog, a very violent dog **kiddies** ● children **the whole slam** ● *A.E.* everything cf. a grand slam in whist or bridge = 13 tricks

AUSTIN: You could spend a couple days. See how you like it. I've got an extra room.

LEE: Too cold up there.

(*Pause*)

AUSTIN: You want to sleep for a while?

LEE: (*Pause, stares at* AUSTIN) I don't sleep.

(*Lights to black.*)

Scene Two

Morning, AUSTIN *is watering plants with a vaporizer,* LEE *sits at glass table in alcove drinking beer.*

LEE: I never realized the old lady was so security-minded.

AUSTIN: How do you mean?

LEE: Made a little tour this morning. She's got locks on everything. Locks and double-locks and chain-locks and—What's she got that's so valuable?

AUSTIN: Antiques I guess. I don't know.

LEE: Antiques! Brought everything with her from the old place, huh. Just the same crap we always had around. Plates and spoons.

AUSTIN: I guess they have personal value to her.

LEE: Personal value. Yeah. Just a lota' junk. Most of it's phony anyway. Idaho decals. Now who in the hell wants to eat offa' plate with the State of Idaho starin' ya' in the face. Every time ya' take a bite ya' get to see a little bit more.

AUSTIN: Well it must mean something to her or she wouldn't save it.

LEE: Yeah, well personally I don't wanna' be invaded by Idaho when I'm eatin'. When I'm eatin' I'm home. Ya' know what I'm sayin'? I'm not driftin', I'm home. I don't need my thoughts swept off to Idaho. I don't need that!

(*Pause*)

AUSTIN: Did you go out last night?

LEE: Why?

AUSTIN: I thought I heard you go out.

LEE: Yeah, I went out. What about it?

AUSTIN: Just wondered.

vaporizer ['veɪpəraɪzə] *G.* Wasserzerstäuber **antiques** [æn'tiːks] valuable, old things **I guess** *A.E.* I think **crap** △ things of no value **junk** useless things, usually of poor quality **phony** imitation **Idaho** state in U.S.A. **decals** ['diːkælz] (decalcomania) *G.* Abziehbilder **to take a bite** ● to put s.th. in one's mouth **to drift** to wander around aimlessly **to sweep off** to carry away suddenly

LEE: Damn coyotes kept me awake.

AUSTIN: Oh yeah, I heard them. They must've killed somebody's dog or something.

LEE: Yappin' their fool heads off. They don't yap like that on the desert. They howl. These are city coyotes here.

AUSTIN: Well, you don't sleep anyway do you?

(*Pause,* LEE *stares at him.*)

LEE: You're pretty smart aren't ya'?

AUSTIN: How do you mean?

LEE: I mean you never had any more on the ball than I did. But here you are gettin' invited into prominent people's houses. Sittin' around talkin' like you know somethin'.

AUSTIN: They're not so prominent.

LEE: They're a helluva' lot more prominent than the houses I get invited into.

AUSTIN: Well you invite yourself.

LEE: That's right. I do. In fact I probably got a wider range a' choices than you do, come to think of it.

AUSTIN: I wouldn't doubt it.

LEE: In fact I been inside some pretty classy places in my time. And I never even went to an Ivy League school either.

AUSTIN: You want some breakfast or something?

LEE: Breakfast?

AUSTIN: Yeah. Don't you eat breakfast?

LEE: Look, don't worry about me pal. I can take care a' myself. You just go ahead as though I wasn't even here, all right?

(AUSTIN *goes into kitchen, makes coffee.*)

AUSTIN: Where'd you walk to last night?

(*Pause*)

LEE: I went up in the foothills there. Up in the San Gabriels. Heat was drivin' me crazy.

AUSTIN: Well, wasn't it hot out on the desert?

LEE: Different kinda' heat. Out there it's clean. Cools off at night. There's a nice little breeze.

AUSTIN: Where were you, the Mojave?

to yap one's head off to bark loudly for a long time without interruption **pretty smart** ● rather clever **on the ball** △ learning, intelligence, ability **ball** △ *here:* head **range** selection **to doubt** *G.* bezweifeln **classy** ● exclusive **Ivy League school** *A.E.* group of colleges in the New England states in the U.S.A. **pal** ● close friend **to go ahead** to continue **foothills** *here:* low hills near the Sierra Nevada in California **San Gabriels** now part of Los Angeles **breeze** light, gentle wind **Mojave** famous desert east of Los Angeles near Nevada

LEE: Yeah. The Mojave. That's right.

AUSTIN: I haven't been out there in years.

LEE: Out past Needles there.

AUSTIN: Oh yeah.

LEE: Up here it's different. This country's real different.

AUSTIN: Well, it's been built up.

LEE: Built up? Wiped out is more like it. I don't even hardly recognize it.

AUSTIN: Yeah. Foothills are the same though, aren't they?

LEE: Pretty much. It's funny goin' up in there. The smells and everything. Used to catch snakes up there, remember?

AUSTIN: You caught snakes.

LEE: Yeah. And you'd pretend you were Geronimo or some damn thing. You used to go right out to lunch.

AUSTIN: I enjoyed my imagination.

LEE: That what you call it? Looks like yer still enjoyin' it.

AUSTIN: So you just wandered around up there, huh?

LEE: Yeah. With a purpose.

AUSTIN: See any houses?

(*Pause*)

LEE: Couple. Couple a' real nice ones. One of 'em didn't even have a dog. Walked right up and stuck my head in the window. Not a peep. Just a sweet kinda' suburban silence.

AUSTIN: What kind of place was it?

LEE: Like a paradise. Kinda' place that sorta' kills ya' inside. Warm yellow lights. Mexican tile all around. Copper pots hangin' over the stove. Ya' know like they got in the magazines. Blond people movin' in and outa' the rooms, talkin' to each other. (*Pause*) Kinda place you wish you'd sorta' grew up in, ya' know.

AUSTIN: That's the kind of place you wish you'd grown up in?

LEE: Yeah, why not?

AUSTIN: I thought you hated that kind of stuff.

LEE: Yeah, well you never knew too much about me did ya'?

(*Pause*)

AUSTIN: Why'd you go out to the desert in the first place?

LEE: I was on my way to see the old man.

AUSTIN: You mean you just passed through there?

Needles town on the border between Los Angeles and the Nevada desert **to wipe out** *G.* auslöschen **pretty much** almost **Geronimo** Apache Indian chief 1829?–1909, a strong leader **purpose** *G.* Ziel **peep** ● sound **tile** *G.* Kacheln, Fliesen **copper** *G.* Kupfer **in the first place** *G.* überhaupt

LEE: Yeah. That's right. Three months of passin' through.

AUSTIN: Three months?

LEE: Somethin' like that. Maybe more. Why?

AUSTIN: You lived on the Mojave for three months?

LEE: Yeah. What'sa' matter with that?

AUSTIN: By yourself?

LEE: Mostly. Had a couple a' visitors. Had that dog for a while.

AUSTIN: Didn't you miss people?

LEE: (*Laughs*) People?

AUSTIN: Yeah. I mean I go crazy if I have to spend three nights in a motel by myself.

LEE: Yer not in a motel now.

AUSTIN: No, I know. But sometimes I have to stay in motels.

LEE: Well, they got people in motels don't they?

AUSTIN: Strangers.

LEE: Yer friendly aren't ya'? Aren't you the friendly type?

(*Pause*)

AUSTIN: I'm going to have somebody coming by here later, Lee.

LEE: Ah! Lady friend?

AUSTIN: No, a producer.

LEE: Aha! What's he produce?

AUSTIN: Film. Movies. You know.

LEE: Oh, movies. Motion Pictures! A Big Wig huh?

AUSTIN: Yeah.

LEE: What's he comin' by here for?

AUSTIN: We have to talk about a project.

LEE: Whadya' mean, 'a project'? What's 'a project'?

AUSTIN: A script.

LEE: Oh. That's what yer doin' with all these papers?

AUSTIN: Yeah.

LEE: Well, what's the project about?

AUSTIN: We're uh—It's a period piece.

LEE: What's 'a period piece'?

AUSTIN: Look, it doesn't matter. The main thing is we need to discuss this alone. I mean—

LEE: Oh, I get it. You want me outa' the picture.

AUSTIN: Not exactly. I just need to be alone with him for a couple of hours. So we can talk.

to miss people to feel lonely **Big Wig (= Big Wheel)** ● important or influential person, e.g. a director **period piece** historical **main** most important

LEE: Yer afraid I'll embarrass ya' huh?

AUSTIN: I'm not afraid you'll embarrass me!

LEE: Well, I tell ya' what—Why don't you just gimme the keys to yer car and I'll be back around six o'clock or so. That give ya enough time?

AUSTIN: I'm not loaning you my car, Lee.

LEE: You want me to just git lost, huh? Take a hike? Is that it? Pound the pavement for a few hours while you bullshit yer way into a million bucks.

AUSTIN: Look, it's going to be hard enough for me to face this character on my own without—

LEE: You don't know this guy?

AUSTIN: No I don't know—He's a producer. I mean I've been meeting with him for months but you never get to know a producer.

LEE: Yer tryin' to hustle him? Is that it?

AUSTIN: I'm not trying to hustle him! I'm trying to work out a deal! It's not easy.

LEE: What kinda' deal?

AUSTIN: Convince him it's a worthwhile story.

LEE: He's not convinced? How come he's comin' over here if he's not convinced? I'll convince him for ya'.

AUSTIN: You don't understand the way things work down here.

LEE: How do things work down here?

(*Pause*)

AUSTIN: Look, if I loan you my car will you have it back here by six?

LEE: On the button. With a full tank a' gas.

AUSTIN: (*Digging in his pocket for keys*) Forget about the gas.

LEE: Hey, these days gas is gold, old buddy.

(AUSTIN *hands the keys to* LEE.)

You remember that car I used to loan you?

AUSTIN: Yeah.

LEE: Forty Ford. Flathead.

AUSTIN: Yeah.

LEE: Sucker hauled ass didn't it?

to embarrass [ɪm'bærəs] to make s.o. feel uncomfortable in front of others **to take a hike** ● to go away for a while **to pound the pavement** to walk along the streets for a long time **bullshit** △ Kraftausdruck **bucks** *A.E.* dollars **to face** to meet with courage **to hustle** *A.E.* to make money in a dishonest way **deal** business agreement **to convince** to persuade s.o. to believe s.th. **worthwhile** *G.* lohnend **on the button** ● *A.E.* punctually, exact time **tank** petrol container in a car **gas** *A.E.* petrol **buddy** ● *A.E.* companion, friend **Forty Ford** Nineteen-Forty Ford. One of the best Fords built before WW II **Flathead** the word describes the shape of the engine **sucker hauled ass** [hɔːld] △ the car drove very fast

AUSTIN: Lee, it's not that I don't want to loan you my car—

LEE: You are loanin' me yer car.

(LEE *gives* AUSTIN *a pat on the shoulder. Pause*)

AUSTIN: I know. I just wish—

LEE: What? You wish what?

AUSTIN: I don't know. I wish I wasn't—I wish I didn't have to be doing business down here. I'd like to just spend some time with you.

LEE: I thought it was "Art" you were doin'.

(LEE *moves across the kitchen toward exit, tosses keys in his hand.*)

AUSTIN: Try to get it back here by six, okay?

LEE: No sweat. Hey, ya' know, if that uh—story of yours doesn't go over with the guy—tell him I got a couple a' 'projects' he might be interested in. Real commercial. Full a' suspense. True-to-life stuff.

(LEE *exits,* AUSTIN *stares after him then turns, goes to papers at table, leafs through pages, lights fade to black.*)

Scene Three

Afternoon, alcove, SAUL KIMMER *and* AUSTIN *seated across from each other at table.*

SAUL: Well, to tell you the truth, Austin, I have never felt so confident about a project in quite a long time.

AUSTIN: Well, that's good to hear, Saul.

SAUL: I am absolutely convinced we can get this thing off the ground. I mean we'll have to make a sale to television and that means getting a major star. Somebody bankable. But I think we can do it. I really do.

AUSTIN: Don't you think we need a first draft before we approach a star?

SAUL: No, no, not at all. I don't think it's necessary. Maybe a brief synopsis. I don't want you to touch the typewriter until we have some seed money.

AUSTIN: That's fine with me.

SAUL: I mean it's a great story. Just the story alone. You've really managed to capture something this time.

pat quick, gentle tap or touch **to toss** to throw gently into the air **no sweat** ● *A.E.* don't worry, no problem **to go over** ● to be liked **suspense** state of uncertainty and expectation **to leaf through** to turn over the pages **to fade** to lose colour slowly **confident** certain about s.th. **to get s.th. off the ground** to start s.th. new, get s.th. started **bankable** s.o. who is so well-known that people would like to see him appear in a play and would pay money to do so **draft** rough outline of a story, notes **to approach** *here:* to make an offer **synopsis** [sɪˈnɒpsɪs] summary, overview **seed money** *A.E.* money to begin financing a project **to manage** to be able to **to capture** to describe s.th. exactly

AUSTIN: I'm glad you like it, Saul.

(LEE *enters abruptly into kitchen carrying a stolen television set. Short pause.*)

LEE: Aw shit, I'm sorry about that. I am really sorry, Austin.

AUSTIN: (*Standing*) That's all right.

LEE: (*Moving toward them*) I mean I thought it was way past six already. You said to have it back here by six.

AUSTIN: We were just finishing up. (*To* SAUL.) This is my uh—brother, Lee.

SAUL: (*Standing*) Oh, I'm very happy to meet you.

(LEE *sets TV on sink counter, shakes hands with* SAUL.)

LEE: I can't tell ya' how happy I am to meet you, sir.

SAUL: Saul Kimmer.

LEE: Mr Kipper.

SAUL: Kimmer.

AUSTIN: Lee's been living out on the desert and he just uh—

SAUL: Oh, that's terrific! (To LEE.) Palm Springs?

LEE: Yeah. Yeah, right. Right around in that area. Near uh—Bob Hope Drive there.

SAUL: Oh I love it out there. I just love it. The air is wonderful.

LEE: Yeah. Sure is. Healthy.

SAUL: And the golf. I don't know if you play golf, but the golf is just about the best.

LEE: I play a lota' golf.

SAUL: Is that right?

LEE: Yeah. In fact I was hoping I'd run into somebody out here who played a little golf. I've been lookin' for a partner.

SAUL: Well, I uh—

AUSTIN: Lee's just down for a visit while our mother's in Alaska.

SAUL: Oh, your mother's in Alaska?

AUSTIN: Yes. She went up there on a little vacation. This is her place.

SAUL: I see. Well isn't that something. Alaska.

LEE: What kinda' handicap do ya' have, Mr Kimmer?

SAUL: Oh I'm just a Sunday duffer really. You know.

LEE: That's good 'cause I haven't swung a club in months.

SAUL: Well we ought to get together sometime and have a little game. Austin, do you play? (SAUL *mimes a Johnny Carson golf swing for* AUSTIN.)

way past *A.E.* a long time after **to finish up** *A.E.* to come to the end of s.th. **Kipper** *G.* Räucherhering **Palm Springs** millionaires' holiday oasis in southern California **Bop Hope** famous film comedian **Drive** road **to run into s.o.** to meet s.o. by chance **something** ● amazing, incredible **Sunday duffer** not a very good golf player (plays golf only on Sundays) **to swing a club** ● to play golf **Johnny Carson** a famous TV-entertainer who often on his programme imitates a golf swing

AUSTIN: No. I don't uh—I've watched it on TV.

LEE: (*To* SAUL) How 'bout tomorrow morning? Bright and early. We could get out there and put in eighteen holes before breakfast.

SAUL: Well, I've got uh—I have several appointments—

LEE: No, I mean real early. Crack a' dawn. While the dew's still thick on the fairway.

SAUL: Sounds really great.

LEE: Austin could be our caddie.

SAUL: Now that's an idea. (*Laughs*) / malicious

AUSTIN: I don't know the first thing about golf.

LEE: There's nothin' to it. Isn't that right, Saul? He'd pick it up in fifteen minutes.

SAUL: Sure. Doesn't take long. 'Course you have to play for years to find your true form. (*Chuckles*)

LEE: (*To* AUSTIN) We'll give ya' a quick run-down on the club faces. The irons, the woods. Show ya' a couple pointers on the basic swing. Might even let ya' hit the ball a couple times. Whadya' think, Saul?

SAUL: Why not. I think it'd be great. I haven't had any exercise in weeks.

LEE: 'At's the spirit! We'll have a little orange juice right afterwards. (*Pause*)

SAUL: Orange juice?

LEE: Yeah! Vitamin C! Nothin' like a shot a' orange juice after a round a' golf. Hot shower. Snappin' towels at each other's privates. Real sense a' fraternity.

SAUL: (*Smiles at* AUSTIN) Well, you make it sound very inviting, I must say. It really does sound great. / hopeful / friendly

LEE: Then it's a date.

SAUL: Well, I'll call the country club and see if I can arrange something. / helpful

LEE: Great! Boy, I sure am sorry that I busted in on ya' all in the middle of yer meeting.

SAUL: Oh that's quite all right. We were just about finished anyway.

hopeful

to put in eighteen holes ● to play a round of golf **crack a' dawn** very early **dew** *G.* Tau **fairway** part of the golf course between the greens, usually several hundred yards long, with fairly short grass **caddie** person who carries a golfer's clubs for him **there's nothing to it** it's easy **to pick up** to learn (by playing) **to chuckle** to laugh quietly to oneself **run-down** ● outline, description **club face** bottom part of a golf club **the woods** golf club faces made of wood **pointers** ● tips, practical instructions **'at's the spirit** that's the right attitude **spirit** *G.* Einstellung **shower** *G.* Dusche **to snap** to hit as with a whip **privates** ● genitals **sense of** feeling of **real sense a' fraternity** refers to initiations given to new members joining clubs in colleges **then it's a date** *G.* abgemacht **to bust in on s.o.** ● *A.E.* to interrupt

LEE: I can wait out in the other room if you want.

SAUL: No really—

LEE: Just got Austin's color TV back from the shop. I can watch a little amateur boxing now.

(LEE *and* AUSTIN *exchange looks.*)

SAUL: Oh—Yes.

LEE: You don't fool around in Television, do you Saul?

SAUL: Uh—I have in the past. Produced some TV Specials. Network stuff. But it's mainly features now.

LEE: That's where the big money is, huh?

SAUL: Yes. That's right.

AUSTIN: Why don't I call you tomorrow, Saul, and we'll get together. We can have lunch or something.

SAUL: That'd be terrific.

LEE: Right after the golf.

(*Pause*)

SAUL: What?

LEE: You can have lunch right after the golf.

SAUL: Oh, right.

LEE: Austin was tellin' me that yer interested in stories.

SAUL: Well, we develop certain projects that we feel have commercial potential.

LEE: What kinda' stuff do ya' go in for?

SAUL: Oh, the usual. You know. Good love interest. Lots of action. (*Chuckles at* AUSTIN.)

LEE: Westerns?

SAUL: Sometimes.

AUSTIN: I'll give you a ring, Saul.

(AUSTIN *tries to move* SAUL *across the kitchen but* LEE *blocks their way.*)

LEE: I got a Western that'd knock yer lights out.

SAUL: Oh really?

LEE: Yeah. Contemporary Western. Based on a true story. 'Course I'm not a writer like my brother here. I'm not a man of the pen.

SAUL: Well—

LEE: I mean I can tell ya' a story off the tongue but I can't put it down on paper. That don't make any difference though does it?

to fool around ● to behave foolishly, stupidly **TV special** as opposed to a regular/serial show; soap opera; is normally televised only once **network** *G.* Netz **features** full length cinema pictures **to go in for** to be interested in **that'd knock yer lights out** △ *G.* es würde dich umhauen (begeistern) **to tell a story off the tongue** ● to narrate from memory

SAUL: No, not really.

LEE: I mean plenty a' guys have stories don't they? True-life stories. Musta' been a lota' movies made from real life.

SAUL: Yes. I suppose so.

LEE: I haven't seen a good Western since *Lonely are the Brave*. You remember that movie?

SAUL: No, I'm afraid I—

LEE: Kirk Douglas. Helluva' movie. You remember that movie, Austin?

AUSTIN: Yes.

LEE: (*To* SAUL) The man dies for the love of a horse.

SAUL: Is that right.

LEE: Yeah. Ya' hear the horse screamin' at the end of it. Rain's comin' down. Horse is screamin'. Then there's a shot. BLAM! Just a single shot like that. Then nothin' but the sound of rain. And Kirk Douglas is ridin' in the ambulance. Ridin' away from the scene of the accident. And when he hears that shot he knows that his horse has died. He knows. And you see his eyes. And his eyes die. Right inside his face. And then his eyes close. And you know that he's died too. You know that Kirk Douglas has died from the death of his horse.

SAUL: (*Eyes* AUSTIN *nervously*) Well, it sounds like a great movie. I'm sorry I missed it.

LEE: Yeah, you shouldn't a' missed that one.

SAUL: I'll have to try to catch it some time. Arrange a screening or something. Well, Austin, I'll have to hit the freeway before rush hour.

AUSTIN: (*Ushers* SAUL *toward exit*) It's good seeing you, Saul.

(AUSTIN *and* SAUL *shake hands.*)

LEE: So ya' think there's room for a real Western these days? A true-to-life Western?

SAUL: Well, I don't see why not. Why don't you uh—tell the story to Austin and have him write a little outline.

LEE: You'd take a look at it then?

SAUL: Yes. Sure. I'll give it a read-through. Always eager for new material. (*Smiles at* AUSTIN.)

LEE: That's great! You'd really read it then, huh?

SAUL: It would just be my opinion of course.

plenty a' guys ● *A.E.* a lot of people **Lonely are the Brave** a famous American movie (1962), starring Kirk Douglas, directed by David Miller **Kirk Douglas** famous film star **to scream** *G.* schreien **to shoot** *G.* schießen **to catch it** ● *here:* to see it **to arrange** to organize **to screen a film** to show a film **I'll have to hit the freeway** ● *A.E.* I must leave **freeway** *A.E.* wide, high-speed road **to give s.th. a read-through** to read through quickly

LEE: That's all I want. Just an opinion. I happen to think it has a lota' possibilities.

SAUL: Well, it was great meeting you and I'll—

(SAUL *and* LEE *shake.*)

LEE: I'll call you tomorrow about the golf.

SAUL: Oh. Yes, right.

LEE: Austin's got your number, right?

SAUL: Yes.

LEE: So long, Saul.

(LEE *gives* SAUL *a pat on the back.* SAUL *exits,* AUSTIN *turns to* LEE, *looks at TV, then back to* LEE.)

AUSTIN: Give me the keys.

(AUSTIN *extends his hand toward* LEE, LEE *doesn't move, just stares at* AUSTIN, *smiles. Lights to black.*)

Scene Four

Night, coyotes in distance, fade, sound of typewriter in dark, crickets, candlelight in alcove, dim light in kitchen. Lights reveal AUSTIN *at glass table typing,* LEE *sits across from him, foot on table, drinking beer and whiskey; the TV is still on sink counter,* AUSTIN *types for a while then stops.*

LEE: All right, now read it back to me.

AUSTIN: I'm not reading it back to you, Lee. You can read it when we're finished. I can't spend all night on this.

LEE: You got better things to do?

AUSTIN: Let's just go ahead. Now what happens when he leaves Texas?

LEE: Is he ready to leave Texas yet? I didn't know we were that far along. He's not ready to leave Texas.

AUSTIN: He's right at the border.

LEE: (*Sitting up*) No, see, this is one a' the crucial parts. Right here. (*Taps paper with beer can.*) We can't rush through this. He's not right at the border. He's a good fifty miles from the border. A lot can happen in fifty miles.

AUSTIN: It's only an outline. We're not writing an entire script now.

LEE: Well ya' can't leave things out even if it is an outline. It's one a' the most important parts. Ya' can't go leavin' it out.

so long *A.E.* goodbye **to reveal** to show **to type** *G.* Schreibmaschine schreiben **to spend time** to stay **to go ahead** to begin **crucial** ['kru:ʃl] most important **to rush through s.th.** to do s.th. too quickly **right at** at that exact place **entire** complete, whole

AUSTIN: Okay, okay. Let's just—get it done.

LEE: All right. Now. He's in the truck and he's got his horse trailer and his horse.

AUSTIN: We've already established that.

LEE: And he sees this other guy comin' up behind him in another truck. And that truck is pullin' a gooseneck.

AUSTIN: What's a gooseneck?

LEE: Cattle trailer. You know the kind with a gooseneck, goes right down in the bed a' the pick-up.

AUSTIN: Oh. All right. (*Types*)

LEE: It's important.

AUSTIN: Okay. I got it.

LEE: All these details are important.

(AUSTIN *types as they talk.*)

AUSTIN: I've got it.

LEE: And this other guy's got his horse all saddled up in the back a' the gooseneck.

AUSTIN: Right.

LEE: So both these guys have got their horses right along with 'em, see.

AUSTIN: I understand.

LEE: Then this first guy suddenly realizes two things.

AUSTIN: The guy in front?

LEE: Right. The guy in front realizes two things almost at the same time. Simultaneous.

AUSTIN: What were the two things?

LEE: Number one, he realizes that the guy behind him is the husband of the woman he's been— (LEE *makes gesture of screwing by pumping his arm.*)

AUSTIN: (*Sees* LEE*'s gesture*) Oh. Yeah.

LEE: And number two, he realizes he's in the middle of Tornado Country.

AUSTIN: What's 'Tornado Country'?

LEE: Panhandle.

AUSTIN: Panhandle?

LEE: Sweetwater. Around in that area. Nothin'. Nowhere. And number three—

truck *A.E.* lorry **to establish** *G.* feststellen **gooseneck** ['gu:snek] constructed lower to the ground, needs a high hook to be attached to the truck that pulls it **cattle trailer** enclosed truck without an engine in which they store cattle for transportation **to go right down in the bed** ● *A.E.* to fit exactly **pick-up** *A.E.* small, open truck with low sides **to saddle up** ● *A.E.* to get ready **to screw** △ to have sexual intercourse **Tornado Country** Tornados go through there more often than anywhere else **Panhandle** section of what a part of Texas looks like on the map **Sweetwater** (name of town)

AUSTIN: I thought there was only two.

LEE: There's three. There's a third unforeseen realization.

AUSTIN: And what's that?

LEE: That he's runnin' outa' gas.

AUSTIN: (*Stops typing*) Come on, Lee. (*He gets up, moves to kitchen, gets a glass of water.*)

LEE: Whadya' mean, 'come on'? That's what it is. Write it down! He's runnin' outa' gas.

AUSTIN: It's too—

LEE: What? It's too what? It's too real! That's what ya' mean isn't it ? It's too much like real life!

AUSTIN: It's not like real life! It's not enough like real life. Things don't happen like that.

LEE: What! Men don't fuck other men's women?

AUSTIN: Yes. But they don't end up chasing each other across the Panhandle. Through 'Tornado Country'.

LEE: They do in this movie!

AUSTIN: And they don't have horses conveniently along with them when they run out of gas! And they don't run out of gas either!

LEE: These guys run outa' gas! This is my story and one a' these guys runs outa' gas!

AUSTIN: It's just a dumb excuse to get them into a chase scene. It's contrived.

LEE: It is a chase scene! It's already a chase scene. They been chasin' each other fer days.

AUSTIN: So now they're supposed to abandon their trucks, climb on their horses and chase each other into the mountains?

LEE: (*Standing suddenly*) There aren't any mountains in the Panhandle! It's flat!! (*He turns violently toward windows in alcove and throws beer can at them.*) Goddamn these crickets! (*Yells at crickets.*) Shut up out there! (*Pause, turns back toward table.*) This place is like a fuckin' rest home here. How're you supposed to think!

AUSTIN: You wanna' take a break!

LEE: No, I don't wanna' take a break! I wanna' get this done! This is my last chance to get this done.

AUSTIN: (*Moves back into alcove*) All right. Take it easy.

LEE: I'm gonna' be leavin' this area. I don't have time to mess around here.

to run out of gas to have no petrol left **to fuck** △ to have sexual intercourse **conveniently** [kən'vi:nɪəntlɪ] by pure chance **dumb** ● *A.E.* stupid **contrived** artificial **to abandon** to leave behind **rest home** home for old people **to get s.th. done** to finish **area** this part of the country **to mess around** ● to waste time

AUSTIN: Where are you going?

LEE: Never mind where I'm goin'! That's got nothin' do to with you. I just gotta' get this done. I'm not like you. Hangin' around bein' a parasite offa' other fools. I gotta' do this thing and get out.

(*Pause*)

AUSTIN: A parasite? Me?

LEE: Yeah, you!

AUSTIN: After you break into people's houses and take their televisions?

LEE: They don't need their televisions! I'm doin' them a service.

AUSTIN: Give me back my keys, Lee.

LEE: Not until you write this thing! You're gonna' write this outline thing for me or that car's gonna wind up in Arizona with a different paint job.

AUSTIN: You think you can force me to write this? I was doing you a favor.

LEE: Git off yer high horse will ya'! Favor! Big favor. Handin' down favors from the mountain top.

AUSTIN: Let's just write it, okay? Let's sit down and not get upset and see if we can just get through this.

(AUSTIN *sits at typewriter. Long pause.*)

LEE: Yer not gonna' even show it to him, are ya'?

AUSTIN: What?

LEE: This outline. You got no intention of showin' it to him. Yer just doin' this 'cause yer afraid a' me.

AUSTIN: You can show it to him yourself.

LEE: I will, boy! I'm gonna' read it to him on the golf course.

AUSTIN: And I'm not afraid of you either.

LEE: Then how come yer doin' it?

AUSTIN: (*Pause*) So I can get my keys back.

(*Pause as* LEE *takes keys out of his pocket slowly and throws them on table. Long pause.* AUSTIN *stares at keys.*)

LEE: There. Now you got yer keys back.

(AUSTIN *looks up at* LEE *but doesn't take keys.*)

Go ahead. There's yer keys.

(AUSTIN *slowly takes keys off table and puts them back in his own pocket.*)

Now what're you gonna' do? Kick me out?

AUSTIN: I'm not going to kick you out, Lee.

LEE: You couldn't kick me out, boy.

to do s.o. a service to help s.o. **to wind up** ● to be found **a different paint job** ● a different colour **to get on one's high horse** *G.* sich aufs hohe Roß setzen **to get upset** *G.* sich aufregen **go ahead** *G.* los! **to kick s.o. out** ● to send s.o. away, get rid of s.o.

AUSTIN: I know.

LEE: So you can't even consider that one. (*Pause*) You could call the Police. That'd be the obvious thing.

AUSTIN: You're my brother.

LEE: That don't mean a thing. You go down to the L.A. Police Department there and ask them what kinda' people kill each other most. What do you think they'd say?

AUSTIN: Who said anything about killing?

LEE: Family people. Brothers. Brothers-in-Law. Cousins. Real American-type people. They kill each other in the heat mostly. In the Smog-Alerts. In the Brush-Fire Season. Right about this time a' year.

AUSTIN: This isn't the same.

LEE: Oh no? What makes it different?

AUSTIN: We're not insane. We're not driven to acts of violence like that. Not over a dumb movie script. Now sit down.

(*Long pause,* LEE *considers which way to go with it.*)

LEE: Maybe not. (*He sits back down at table across from* AUSTIN.) Maybe you're right. Maybe we're too intelligent, huh? (*Pause*) We got our heads on our shoulders. One of us has even got a Ivy League diploma. Now that means somethin' don't it? Doesn't that mean somethin'?

AUSTIN: Look, I'll write this thing for you, Lee. I don't mind writing it. I just don't want to get all worked up about it. It's not worth it. Now, come on. Let's just get through it, okay?

LEE: Nah. I think there's easier money. Lotsa' places I could pick up thousands. Maybe millions. I don't need this shit. I could go up to Sacramento Valley and steal me a diesel. Ten thousand a week dismantling one a' those suckers. Ten thousand a week! (*He opens another beer, puts his foot back up on table.*)

AUSTIN: No, really, look, I'll write it out for you. I think it's a great idea.

LEE: Nah, you got yer own work to do. I don't wanna' interfere with yer life.

AUSTIN: I mean it'd be really fantastic if you could sell this. Turn it into a movie. I mean it.

(*Pause*)

LEE: Ya' think so, huh?

one *here:* idea **obvious** clear, easily understood **L.A. Police Department** the police in Los Angeles **smog alert** [əˈlɜːt] smog alarm **brush-fire season** dry time of year when forest fires break out **insane** [ɪnˈseɪn] mad, mentally ill **to have one's head on one's shoulders** to have practical ability, common sense **Sacramento Valley** a huge valley in California stretching from north to south **diesel** car or lorry using diesel petrol **to dismantle** to take apart **sucker** △ Kraftausdruck, *G.* Dinge (can be used for anything) **to interfere** [ˌɪntəˈfɪə(r)] *G.* sich einmischen

AUSTIN: Absolutely. You could really turn your life around, you know. Change things.

LEE: I could get me a house maybe.

AUSTIN: Sure you could get a house. You could get a whole ranch if you wanted to.

LEE: (*Laughs*) A ranch? I could get a ranch?

AUSTIN: 'Course you could. You know what a screenplay sells for these days?

LEE: No. What's it sell for?

AUSTIN: A lot. A whole lot of money.

LEE: Thousands?

AUSTIN: Yeah. Thousands.

LEE: Millions?

AUSTIN: Well—

LEE: We could get the old man outa' hock then.

AUSTIN: Maybe.

LEE: Maybe? Whadya' mean, maybe?

AUSTIN: I mean it might take more than money.

LEE: You were just tellin' me it'd change my whole life around. Why wouldn't it change his?

AUSTIN: He's different.

LEE: Oh, he's of a different ilk, huh?

AUSTIN: He's not gonna' change. Let's leave the old man out of it.

LEE: That's right. He's not gonna' change but I will. I'll just turn myself right inside out. I could be just like you then, huh? Sittin' around dreamin' stuff up. Gettin' paid to dream. Ridin' back and forth on the freeway just dreamin' my fool head off.

AUSTIN: It's not all that easy.

LEE: It's not, huh?

AUSTIN: No. There's a lot of work involved.

LEE: What's the toughest part? Deciding whether to jog or play tennis? (*Long pause.*)

AUSTIN: Well, look. You can stay here—do whatever you want to. Borrow the car. Come in and out. Doesn't matter to me. It's not my house. I'll help you write this thing or—not. Just let me know what you want. You tell me.

LEE: Oh. So now suddenly you're at my service. Is that it?

AUSTIN: What do you want to do, Lee?

screenplay script for a film **s.th. sells for** s.th. can be sold for **a whole lot** ● *A.E.* a very large sum of money **I am in hock to s.o.** I owe money to s.o. **he is of a different ilk** he is different, he is not the same as others **stuff** ● ideas **back and forth** *G.* hin und her **dreaming my fool head off** ● thinking up ideas (serious ideas, not fantasies here) **toughest** most difficult

(*Long pause.* LEE *stares at him then turns and dreams at windows.*)

LEE: I tell ya' what I'd do if I still had that dog. Ya' wanna' know what I'd do?

AUSTIN: What?

LEE: Head out to Ventura. Cook up a little match. God that little dog could bear down. Lota' money in dog fightin'. Big money.

(*Pause*)

AUSTIN: Why don't we try to see this through, Lee. Just for the hell of it. Maybe you've really got something here. What do you think?

(*Pause.* LEE *considers.*)

LEE: Maybe so. No harm in tryin' I guess. You think it's such a hot idea. Besides, I always wondered what'd be like to be you.

AUSTIN: You did?

LEE: Yeah, sure. I used to picture you walkin' around some campus with yer arms fulla' books. Blondes chasin' after ya'.

AUSTIN: Blondes? That's funny.

LEE: What's funny about it?

AUSTIN: Because I always used to picture you somewhere.

LEE: Where'd you picture me?

AUSTIN: Oh, I don't know. Different places. Adventures. You were always on some adventure.

LEE: Yeah.

AUSTIN: And I used to say to myself, "Lee's got the right idea. He's out there in the world and here I am. What am I doing?"

LEE: Well you were settin' yourself up for somethin'.

AUSTIN: I guess.

LEE: We better get started on this thing then.

AUSTIN: Okay. (*He sits up at typewriter, puts new paper in.*)

LEE: Oh. Can I get the keys back before I forget?

(AUSTIN *hesitates.*)

You said I could borrow the car if I wanted, right? Isn't that what you said?

AUSTIN: Yeah. Right.

(AUSTIN *takes keys out of his pocket, sets them on table,* LEE *takes keys slowly, plays with them in his hand.*)

LEE: I could get a ranch, huh?

AUSTIN: Yeah. We have to write it first though.

LEE: Okay. Let's write it.

(*Lights start dimming slowly to end of scene as* AUSTIN *types,* LEE *speaks.*)

Ventura city in south west California **to bear down** to attack **for the hell of it** ● for fun **hot** ● clever **to picture s.o. or s.th.** *G.* sich vorstellen **to set oneself up for** to prepare **to dim** to become darker slowly

So they take off after each other straight into an endless black prairie. The sun is just comin' down and they can feel the night on their backs. What they don't know is that each one of 'em is afraid see. Each one separately thinks that he's the only one that's afraid. And they keep ridin' like that straight into the night. Not knowing. And the one who's chasin' doesn't know where the other one is taking him. And the one who's being chased doesn't know where he's going.
(*Lights to black, typing stops in the dark, crickets fade. Music in Act break: Hank Williams' "Ramblin' Man".*)

to take off after s.o. or s.th. to follow, chase **Hank Williams** famous country and western singer (1923–1953) **Ramblin' Man** title of a well-known Hank Williams song

Act Two

Scene Five

Morning, LEE *at table in alcove with a set of golf clubs in a fancy leather bag,* AUSTIN *at sink washing a few dishes.*

AUSTIN: He really liked it, huh?

LEE: He wouldn't a' gave me these clubs if he didn't like it.

AUSTIN: He gave you the clubs?

LEE: Yeah. I told ya' he gave me the clubs. The bag too.

AUSTIN: I thought he just loaned them to you.

LEE: He said it was part a' the advance. A little gift like. Gesture of his good faith.

AUSTIN: He's giving you an advance?

LEE: Now what's so amazing about that? I told ya' it was a good story. You even said it was a good story.

AUSTIN: Well that is really incredible, Lee. You know how many guys spend their whole lives down here trying to break into this business? Just trying to get in the door?

LEE: (*Pulling clubs out of bag, testing them*) I got no idea. How many? (*Pause*)

AUSTIN: How much of an advance is he giving you?

LEE: Plenty. We were talkin' big money out there. Ninth hole is where I sealed the deal.

AUSTIN: He made a firm commitment?

LEE: Absolutely.

AUSTIN: Well, I know Saul and he doesn't fool around when he says he likes something.

LEE: I thought you said you didn't know him.

AUSTIN: Well, I'm familiar with his tastes.

LEE: I let him get two up on me goin' into the back nine. He was sure he had me cold. You shoulda' seen his face when I pulled out the old pitching wedge and plopped it pin-high, two feet from the cup. He 'bout shit his

fancy unusual, brightly coloured **advance** some money payed before work is finished **a gift like** like a little present **good faith** good will **incredible** difficult to believe **to break into** *here:* to have a chance to begin **to seal a deal** ● to bring a business transaction to a successful end **firm commitment** definite promise **to fool around** not take things seriously **to be familiar with** to know quite well **two up on me** two points ahead in the game **back nine** last nine holes on a golf course **to have s.o. cold** ● to beat s.o. easily, win easily **pitching wedge** kind of golf club **plopped it pin-high … cup** hit the ball so that it landed two feet from the hole

pants. "Where'd a guy like you ever learn how to play golf like that?" he says.

(LEE *laughs,* AUSTIN *stares at him.*)

AUSTIN: 'Course there's no contract yet. Nothing's final until it's on paper.

LEE: It's final, all right. There's no way he's gonna' back out of it now. We gambled for it.

AUSTIN: Saul, gambled?

LEE: Yeah, sure. I mean he liked the outline already so he wasn't risking that much. I just guaranteed it with my short game.

(*Pause*)

AUSTIN: Well, we should celebrate or something. I think Mom left a bottle of Champagne in the refrigerator. We should have a little toast.

(AUSTIN *gets glasses from cupboard, goes to refrigerator, pulls out bottle of Champagne.*)

LEE: You shouldn't oughta' take her Champagne, Austin. She's gonna' miss that.

AUSTIN: Oh, she's not going to mind. She'd be glad we put it to good use. I'll get her another bottle. Besides, it's perfect for the occasion.

(*Pause*)

LEE: Yer gonna' get a nice fee fer writin' the script a' course. Straight fee.

(AUSTIN *stops, stares at* LEE, *puts glasses and bottle on table. Pause*)

AUSTIN: I'm writing the script?

LEE: That's what he said. Said we couldn't hire a better screenwriter in the whole town.

AUSTIN: But I'm already working on a script. I've got my own project. I don't have time to write two scripts.

LEE: No, he said he was gonna' drop that other one.

(*Pause*)

AUSTIN: What? You mean mine? He's going to drop mine and do yours instead?

LEE: (*Smiles*) Now look, Austin, it's jest beginner's luck ya' know. I mean I sank a fifty-foot putt for this deal. No hard feelings.

(AUSTIN *goes to phone on wall, grabs it, starts dialing.*)

He's not gonna' be in, Austin. Told me he wouldn't be in 'til late this afternoon.

to back out of s.th. to withdraw from a promise or undertaking **to gamble** to take risks to make or win money **toast** *G.* Trinkspruch **to mind about s.th.** to worry about, object to **to put s.th. to good use** to make good use of **fee** *G.* Honorar **to drop s.th.** ● not use **to sink a putt** [pʌt] to hit the golf ball into the hole **to putt** to hit the golf ball so that it rolls in the direction of the hole **deal** *G.* Geschäft

AUSTIN: (*Stays on phone, dialing, listens*) I can't believe this. I just can't believe it. Are you sure he said that? Why would he drop mine?

LEE: That's what he told me.

AUSTIN: He can't do that without telling me first. Without talking to me at least. He wouldn't just make a decision like that without talking to me!

LEE: Well I was kinda' surprised myself. But he was real enthusiastic about my story.

(AUSTIN *hangs up phone violently, paces.*)

AUSTIN: What'd he say! Tell me everything he said!

LEE: I been tellin' ya'! He said he liked the story a whole lot. It was the first authentic Western to come along in a decade.

AUSTIN: He liked that story? Your story?

LEE: Yeah! What's so surprisin' about that?

AUSTIN: It's stupid! It's the dumbest story I ever heard in my life.

LEE: Hey, hold on! That's my story yer talkin' about!

AUSTIN: It's a bullshit story! It's idiotic. Two lamebrains chasing each other across Texas! Are you kidding? Who do you think's going to go see a film like that?

LEE: It's not a film! It's a movie. There's a big difference. That's somethin' Saul told me.

AUSTIN: Oh he did, huh?

LEE: Yeah, he said, "In this business we make Movies, Amercian Movies. Leave the Films to the French."

AUSTIN: So you got real intimate with old Saul, huh? He started pouring forth his vast knowledge of Cinema.

LEE: I think he liked me a lot, to tell ya' the truth. I think he felt I was somebody he could confide in.

AUSTIN: What'd you do, beat him up or something?

LEE: (*Stands fast*) Hey, I've about had it with the insults, buddy! You think yer the only one in the brain department here? Yer the only one that can sit around and cook things up? There's other people got ideas too, ya' know!

AUSTIN: You must've done something. Threatened him or something. Now what'd you do, Lee?

LEE: I convinced him!

(LEE *makes sudden menacing lunge toward* AUSTIN, *wielding golf club above*

real *A.E.* really, extremely **authentic** *G.* authentisch, echt **to come along** ● appear **decade** ['dekeɪd] period of 10 years **lamebrains** △ complete idiots **lame** *G.* lahm, hinkend **to kid** ● to joke **to pour forth** ● to show **vast** *G.* riesig **to confide in** *G.* (an)vertrauen **to beat s.o. up** to fight and injure s.o. **I've about had it** ● I have had enough **to cook things up** ● to invent new ideas **to threaten** *G.* drohen **menacing** ['menəsɪŋ] threatening **to wield** [wi:ld] to swing around e.g. an axe or sword

his head, stops himself, frozen moment, long pause. LEE *lowers club.*)

AUSTIN: Oh, Jesus. You didn't hurt him did you?

(*Long silence,* LEE *sits back down at table.*)

Lee! Did you hurt him?

LEE: I didn't do nothin' to him! He liked my story. Pure and simple. He said it was the best story he's come across in a long, long time.

AUSTIN: That's what he told me about my story! That's the same thing he said to me.

LEE: Well, he musta' been lyin'. He musta' been lyin' to one of us anyway.

AUSTIN: You can't come into this town and start pushing people around. They're gonna' put you away!

LEE: I never pushed anybody around! I beat him fair and square. (*Pause*) They can't touch me anyway. They can't put a finger on me. I'm gone. I can come in through the window and go out through the door. They never knew what hit 'em. You, yer stuck. Yer the one that's stuck. Not me. So don't be warnin' me what to do in this town.

be honest

(*Pause,* AUSTIN *crosses to table, sits at typewriter, rest.*)

AUSTIN: Lee come, on, level with me will you? It doesn't make any sense that suddenly he'd throw my idea out the window. I've been talking to him for months. I've got too much at stake. Everything's riding on this project.

LEE: What's yer idea?

AUSTIN: It's just a simple love story.

LEE: What kinda' love story?

AUSTIN: (*Stands, crosses into kitchen*) I'm not telling you!

LEE: Ha! 'Fraid I'll steal it, huh? Competition's gettin' kinda' close to home isn't it?

AUSTIN: Where did Saul say he was going?

LEE: He was gonna' take my story to a couple studios.

AUSTIN: That's *my* outline you know! I wrote that outline! You've got no right to be peddling it around.

LEE: You weren't ready to take credit for it last night.

AUSTIN: Give me my keys!

LEE: What?

AUSTIN: The keys! I want my keys back!

LEE: Where you goin'?

musta' been lyin' must have been telling lies **to put s.o. away** ● to send s.o. to prison **to beat s.o. fair and square** ● to win honestly **to be stuck** ● not able to move away **to level with s.o.** ● to be honest with s.o. **to have a lot at stake** to risk a lot **to ride on** ● to depend on **to peddle s.th. around** *G.* hausieren gehen **to take credit for** to accept responsibility/praise

AUSTIN: Just give me my keys! I gotta' take a drive. I gotta' get out of here for a while.

LEE: Where you gonna' go, Austin?

AUSTIN: (*Pause*) I might just drive out to the desert for a while. I gotta' think.

LEE: You can think here just as good. This is the perfect set-up for thinkin'. We got some writin' to do here, boy. Now let's just have us a little toast. Relax. We're partners now.

(LEE *pops the cork of the Champagne bottle, pours two drinks as the lights fade to black.*)

Scene Six

Afternoon, LEE *and* SAUL *in kitchen,* AUSTIN *in alcove.*

LEE: Now you tell him. You tell him, Mr Kipper.

SAUL: Kimmer.

LEE: Kimmer. You tell him what you told me. He don't believe me.

AUSTIN: I don't want to hear it.

SAUL: It's really not a big issue. Austin. I was simply amazed by your brother's story and—

AUSTIN: Amazed? You lost a bet! You gambled with my material!

SAUL: That's really beside the point, Austin. I'm ready to go all the way with your brother's story. I think it has a great deal of merit.

AUSTIN: I don't want to hear about it, okay? Go tell it to the executives! Tell it to somebody who's going to turn it into a package deal or something. A TV series. Don't tell it to me.

SAUL: But I want to continue with your project too, Austin. It's not as though we can't do both. We're big enough for that aren't we?

AUSTIN: "We"? *I* can't do both! I don't know about "we".

LEE: (*To* SAUL) See, what'd I tell ya'. He's totally unsympathetic.

SAUL: Austin, there's no point in our going to another screenwriter for this. It just doesn't make sense. You're brothers. You know each other. There's a familiarity with material that just wouldn't be possible otherwise.

AUSTIN: There's no familiarity with the material! None! I don't know what "Tornado Country" is. I don't know what a "gooseneck" is. And I don't

set-up ● place, surroundings **issue** *G.* Angelegenheit **amazed** astounded **bet** gamble **beside the point** irrelevant **merit** value, worth **executives** directors etc. **to turn s.th. into** to change into s.th. else **package deal** *G.* Pauschalangebot **unsympathetic** ['ʌnˌsɪmpə'θetɪk] not sharing another person's ideas or feelings **no point in** *G.* kein Zweck

want to know! (*Pointing to* LEE.) He's a hustler! He's a bigger hustler than you are! If you can't see that, then—

LEE: (*To* AUSTIN) Hey, now hold on. I didn't have to bring this bone back to you, boy. I persuaded Saul here that you were the right man for the job. You don't have to go throwin' up favors in my face.

AUSTIN: Favors! I'm the one who wrote the fuckin' outline! You can't even spell.

SAUL: (*To* AUSTIN) Your brother told me about the situation with your father. (*Pause*)

AUSTIN: What? (*Looks at* LEE.)

SAUL: That's right. Now we have a clear cut deal here, Austin. We have big studio money standing behind this thing. Just on the basis of your outline.

AUSTIN: (*To* SAUL) What'd he tell you about my father?

SAUL: Well—that he's destitute. He needs money.

LEE: That's right. He does.

(AUSTIN *shakes his head, stares at them both.*)

AUSTIN: (*To* LEE) And this little assignment is supposed to go toward the old man? A charity project? Is that what this is? Did you cook this up on the ninth green too?

SAUL: It's a big slice, Austin.

AUSTIN: (*To* LEE) I gave him money! I already gave him money. You know that. He drank it all up!

LEE: This is a different deal here.

SAUL: We can set up a trust for your father. A large sum of money. It can be doled out to him in parcels so he can't misuse it.

AUSTIN: Yeah, and who's doing the doling?

SAUL: Your brother volunteered.

(AUSTIN *laughs.*)

LEE: That's right. I'll make sure he uses it for groceries.

AUSTIN: (*To* SAUL) I'm not doing this script! I'm not writing this crap for you or anybody else. You can't blackmail me into it. You can't threaten me into it. There's no way I'm doing it. So just give it up. Both of you.

(*Long pause.*)

hustler a bit of a swindler, he makes you think that he is not so good as you, but he may suddenly take your money and show that he is much better than you thought **hold on** ● wait, not so fast **bone** ● *here:* prize, opportunity **destitute** ['destɪtjuːt] living in complete poverty **assignment** *G.* Auftrag **charity** *G.* Almosen **big slice** ● *A.E.* important business deal **to set up a trust for s.o.** to invest a significant sum of money which can be paid in instalments over a long period of time **to dole out** ● to give money in instalments **to volunteer** *G.* sich freiwillig melden **crap** △ complete nonsense **to blackmail** *G.* erpressen

SAUL: Well, that's it then. I mean this is an easy three hundred grand. Just for a first draft. It's incredible, Austin. We've got three different studios all trying to cut each other's throats to get this material. In one morning. That's how hot it is.

AUSTIN: Yeah, well you can afford to give me a percentage on the outline then. And you better get the genius here an agent before he gets burned.

LEE: Saul's gonna' be my agent. Isn't that right, Saul?

SAUL: That's right. (*To* AUSTIN.) Your brother has really got something, Austin. I've been around too long not to recognize it. Raw talent.

AUSTIN: He's got a lota' balls is what he's got. He's taking you right down the river.

SAUL: Three hundred thousand, Austin. Just for a first draft. Now you've never been offered that kind of money before.

AUSTIN: I'm not writing it.

(*Pause*)

grand ● *A.E.* a thousand dollars **to cut each other's throats** ● to use unfair tactics to stop s.o. being successful **he's got a lota' balls** △ he's being very aggressive **to take s.o. down the river** ● to deceive, betray

SAUL: I see. Well—

LEE: We'll just go to another writer then. Right, Saul? Just hire us somebody with some enthusiasm. Somebody who can recognize the value of a good story.

SAUL: I'm sorry about this, Austin.

AUSTIN: Yeah.

SAUL: I mean I was hoping we could continue both things but now I don't see how it's possible.

AUSTIN: So you're dropping my idea altogether. Is that it? Just trade horses in mid-stream? After all these months of meetings.

SAUL: I wish there was another way.

AUSTIN: I've got everything riding on this, Saul. You know that. It's my only shot. If this falls through—

SAUL: I have to go with what my instincts tell me—

AUSTIN: Your instincts!

SAUL: My gut reaction.

AUSTIN: You lost! That's your gut reaction. You lost a gamble. Now you're trying to tell me you like his story? How could you possibly fall for that story? It's as phony as Hopalong Cassidy. What do you see in it? I'm curious.

SAUL: It has the ring of truth, Austin.

AUSTIN: (*Laughs*) Truth?

LEE: It is true.

SAUL: Something about the real West.

AUSTIN: Why? Because it's got horses? Because it's got grown men acting like little boys?

SAUL: Something about the land. Your brother is speaking from experience.

AUSTIN: So am I!

SAUL: But nobody's interested in love these days, Austin. Let's face it.

LEE: That's right.

AUSTIN: (*To* SAUL) He's been camped out on the desert for three months. Talking to cactus. What's he know about what people wanna' see on the screen! I drive on the freeway every day. I swallow the smog. I watch the news in color. I shop in the Safeway. I'm the one who's in touch! Not him!

SAUL: I have to go now, Austin. (*He starts to leave.*)

to trade horses in mid-stream to change one's mind halfway through a project **I've got everything riding on this** I've risked everything I have on this **shot** ● chance, opportunity **to fall through** to be a failure, unsuccessful **gut reaction** ● instinctive reaction **phony** *A.E.* false, fake **Hopalong Cassidy** a cowboy in the old West, who was not a real person **to have the ring of truth** to sound completely true **Safeway** big chain of supermarkets **to be in touch** *G.* auf dem laufenden sein

AUSTIN: There's no such thing as the West anymore! It's a dead issue! It's dried up, Saul, and so are you.

(SAUL *stops and turns to* AUSTIN.)

SAUL: Maybe you're right. But I have to take the gamble, don't I?

AUSTIN: You're a fool to do this, Saul.

SAUL: I've always gone on my hunches. Always. And I've never been wrong. (*To* LEE) I'll talk to you tomorrow, Lee.

LEE: All right, Mr Kimmer.

SAUL: Maybe we could have some lunch.

LEE: Fine with me. (*Smiles at* AUSTIN.)

SAUL: I'll give you a ring.

(SAUL *exits, lights to black as brothers look at each other from a distance.*)

Scene Seven

Night, coyotes, crickets, sound of typewriter in dark, candlelight up on LEE *at typewriter struggling to type with one-finger system,* AUSTIN *sits sprawled out on kitchen floor with whiskey bottle, drunk.*

AUSTIN: (*Singing, from floor*)

Red sails in the sunset
Way out on the blue
Please carry my loved one
Home safely to me

Red sails in the sunset—

LEE: (*Slams fist on table*) Hey! Knock it off will ya'! I'm tryin' to concentrate here.

AUSTIN: (*Laughs*) You're tryin' to concentrate?

LEE: Yeah. That's right.

AUSTIN: Now you're tryin' to concentrate.

LEE: Between you, the coyotes and the crickets a thought don't have much of a chance.

AUSTIN: "Between me, the coyotes and the crickets." What a great title.

LEE: I don't need a title! I need a thought.

AUSTIN: (*Laughs*) A thought! Here's a thought for ya'—

to dry up ● to be of no interest anymore **to go on a hunch** ● to follow one's instincts **hunch** idea based on feeling rather than reason **to struggle** to try hard to do s.th. one finds difficult **to sprawl out** to spread out arms and legs in a relaxed position **way out on the blue** far away on the ocean **knock it off** ● stop doing that!

LEE: I'm not askin' fer yer thoughts! I got my own. I can do this thing on my own.

AUSTIN: You're going to write an entire script on your own?

LEE: That's right.

(*Pause*)

AUSTIN: Here's a thought. Saul Kimmer—

LEE: Shut up will ya'!

AUSTIN: He thinks we're the same person.

LEE: Don't get cute.

AUSTIN: He does! He's lost his mind. Poor old Saul. (*Giggles*)— Thinks we're one and the same.

LEE: Why don't you ease up on that Champagne.

AUSTIN: (*Holding up bottle*) This isn't Champagne anymore. We went through the Champagne a long time ago. This is serious stuff. The days of Champagne are long gone.

LEE: Well go outside and drink it.

AUSTIN: I'm enjoying your company, Lee. For the first time since your arrival I am finally enjoying your company. And now you want me to go outside and drink alone?

LEE: That's right. (*He reads through paper in typewriter, makes an erasure.*)

AUSTIN: You think you'll make more progress if you're alone? You might drive yourself crazy.

LEE: I could have this thing done in a night if I had a little silence.

AUSTIN: Well you'd still have the crickets to contend with. The coyotes. The sounds of the Police Helicopters prowling above the neighborhood. Slashing their searchlights down through the streets. Hunting for the likes of you.

LEE: I'm a screenwriter now! I'm legitimate.

AUSTIN: (*Laughing*) A screenwriter!

LEE: That's right. I'm on salary. That's more'n I can say for you. I got an advance coming.

AUSTIN: This is true. This is very true. An advance. (*Pause*) Well, maybe I oughta' go out and try my hand at your trade. Since you're doing so good at mine.

→ Jobtausch

shut up ● be quiet **don't get cute** ● *A.E.* don't try to be clever **to lose one's mind** to become confused **erasure** [ɪˈreɪʒə(r)] *A.E.* deletion **to contend with** *G.* wetteifern **to prowl** to move around like a wild animal looking for s.th. **to slash** to move s.th. around violently and rapidly, e.g. such as with a sword (*here:* with a light) **legitimate** [lɪˈdʒɪtɪmət] *here:* with a socially acceptable job **salary** *G.* Gehalt **I got an advance** *G.* Vorschuß (I got money paid in advance) **trade** job, profession

LEE: Ha! (*He attempts to type some more but gets the ribbon tangled up, starts trying to rethread it as they continue talking.*)

AUSTIN: Well why not? You don't think I've got what it takes to sneak into people's houses and steal their TVs?

LEE: You couldn't steal a toaster without losin' yer lunch.

(AUSTIN *stands with a struggle, supports himself by the sink.*)

AUSTIN: You don't think I could sneak into somebody's house and steal a toaster?

LEE: Go take a shower or somethin' will ya! (*He gets more tangled up with the typewriter ribbon, pulling it out of the machine as though it was fishing line.*)

AUSTIN: You really don't think I could steal a crumby toaster? How much you wanna' bet I can't steal a toaster! How much? Go ahead! You're a gambler aren't you? Tell me how much yer willing to put on the line. Some part of your big advance? Oh, you haven't got that yet have you. I forgot.

LEE: All right. I'll bet you your car that you can't steal a toaster without gettin' busted.

AUSTIN: You already got my car!

LEE: Okay, your house then.

AUSTIN: What're you gonna' give me! I'm not talkin' about my house and my car, I'm talkin' about what are you gonna' give me. You don't have nothin' to give me.

LEE: I'll give you—shared screen credit. How 'bout that? I'll have it put in the contract that this was written by the both of us.

AUSTIN: I don't want my name on that piece of shit! I want something of value. You got anything of value? You got any tidbits from the desert? Any Rattlesnake bones? I'm not a greedy man. Any little personal treasure will suffice.

LEE: I'm gonna' just kick yer ass out in a minute.

AUSTIN: Oh, so now you're gonna' kick me out! Now I'm the intruder. I'm the one who's invading your precious privacy.

LEE: I'm trying to do some screenwriting here! (*He stands, picks up typewriter, slams it down hard on table. Pause, silence except for crickets.*)

AUSTIN: Well, you got everything you need. You got plenty a' coffee? Groceries. You got a car. A contract. (*Pause*) Might need a new typewriter

to attempt to try **ribbon** *G.* Farbband **to get tangled up** to get in a mess **to rethread** [rɪˈθred] to rewind **to sneak** ● to go quietly and secretly **crumby** [ˈkrʌmɪ] ● useless, valueless, not new **to put on the line** *A.E.* to risk money **gettin' busted** △ being caught **screen credit** names of people working on a film shown at the beginning or end e.g. cameraman, producer etc. **tidbits** ● samples of things; a small, interesting piece of s.th. **rattlesnake** *G.* Klapperschlange **greedy** wanting more than one needs **to suffice** [səˈfaɪs] to be enough **I'll kick yer ass out** △ I'm going to fire (discharge) you **intruder** *G.* Störenfried

ribbon but other than that you're pretty well fixed, I'll just leave ya' alone for a while.

(AUSTIN *tries to steady himself to leave,* LEE *makes a move toward him.*)

LEE: Where you goin'?

AUSTIN: Don't worry about me. I'm not the one to worry about.

(*He weaves toward exit, stops.*)

LEE: What're you gonna' do? Just go wander out into the night?

AUSTIN: I'm gonna' make a little tour.

LEE: Why don't ya' just go to bed for Christ's sake. Yer makin' me sick.

AUSTIN: I can take care a' myself. Don't worry about me.

(AUSTIN *weaves badly in another attempt to exit, he crashes to the floor,* LEE *goes to him but remains standing.*)

LEE: You want me to call your wife for ya' or something?

AUSTIN: (*From floor*) My wife?

LEE: Yeah. I mean maybe she can help ya' out. Talk to ya' or somethin'.

AUSTIN: (*Struggles to stand up again*) She's five hundred miles away. North. North of here. Up in the north country where things are calm. I don't need any help. I'm gonnna' go outside and I'm gonna' steal a toaster. I'm gonna' steal some other stuff too. I might even commit bigger crimes. Bigger than you ever dreamed of. Crimes beyond the imagination!

(AUSTIN *manages to get himself vertical, tries to head for exit again.*)

LEE: Just hang on a minute, Austin.

AUSTIN: Why? What for? You don't need my help, right? You got a handle on the project. Besides, I'm lookin' forward to the smell of the night. The bushes. Orange blossoms. Dust in the driveways. Rain bird sprinklers. Lights in people's houses. You're right about the lights, Lee. Everybody else is livin' the life. Indoors. Safe. This is a Paradise down here. You know that? We're livin' in a Paradise. We've forgotten about that.

LEE: You sound just like the old man now.

AUSTIN: Yeah, well we all sound alike when we're sloshed. We just sorta' echo each other.

LEE: Maybe if we could work on this together we could bring him back out here. Get him settled down some place.

(AUSTIN *turns violently toward* LEE, *takes a swing at him, misses and crashes to the floor again.* LEE *stays standing.*)

AUSTIN: I don't want him out here! I've had it with him! I went all the way out

you're pretty well fixed ● you have got almost everything you want or need **to weave** to move unsteadily **yer makin' me sick** △ you annoy and disgust me **hang on** ● wait a moment **to have a handle on s.th.** to know what one should do and what one is going to understand **rain bird sprinklers** *G.* Rasensprenger **sloshed** [slɒʃt] △ very drunk **to take a swing at s.o.** ● to try to hit s.o.

there! I went out of my way. I gave him money and all he did was play Al Jolson records and spit at me! I gave him money!

(*Pause*)

LEE: Just help me a little with the characters, all right? You know how to do it, Austin.

AUSTIN: (*On floor, laughs*) The characters!

LEE: Yeah. You know. The way they talk and stuff. I can hear it in my head but I can't get it down on paper.

AUSTIN: What characters?

LEE: The guys. The guys in the story.

AUSTIN: Those aren't characters.

LEE: Whatever you call 'em then. I need to write somethin' out.

AUSTIN: Those are illusions of characters.

LEE: I don't give a damn what ya' call 'em! You know what I'm talkin' about!

AUSTIN: Those are fantasies of a long lost boyhood.

LEE: I gotta' write somethin' out on paper!

(*Pause*)

AUSTIN: What for? Saul's gonna' get you a fancy screenwriter isn't he?

LEE: I wanna' do it myself!

AUSTIN: Then do it! Yer on your own now old buddy. You bulldogged yer way into contention. Now you gotta' carry it through.

LEE: I will but I need some advice. Just a couple a' things. Come on, Austin. Just help me get 'em talkin' right. It won't take much.

AUSTIN: Oh, now you're having a little doubt, huh? What happened? The pressure's on, boy. This is it. You gotta' come up with it now. You don't come up with a winner on your first time out they just cut your head off. They don't give you a second chance ya' know.

LEE: I got a good story! I know it's a good story. I just need a little help is all.

AUSTIN: Not from me. Not from yer little old brother. I'm retired.

LEE: You could save this thing for me, Austin. I'd give ya' half the money. I would. I only need half anyway. With this kinda' money I could be a long time down the road. I'd never bother ya' again. I promise. You'd never even see me again.

AUSTIN: (*Still on floor*) You'd disappear?

LEE: I would for sure.

Al Jolson famous singer who starred in the first "talking" picture **stuff** ● *G.* Zeug **I don't give a damn** △ I don't care at all **to bulldog one's way into contention** to push your way forward without considering other people's feelings, to be competitive with other people **the pressure's on** ● the situation is serious, we are getting down to brass tacks **to come up with s.th.** to finish s.th. successfully **to retire** to stop work (usually at or after sixty)

AUSTIN: Where would you disappear to?

LEE: That don't matter. I got plenty a' places.

AUSTIN: Nobody can disappear. The old man tried that. Look where it got him. He lost his teeth.

LEE: He never had any money.

AUSTIN: I don't mean that. I mean his teeth! His real teeth. First he lost his real teeth, then he lost his false teeth. You never knew that did ya'? He never confided in you.

LEE: Nah, I never knew that.

AUSTIN: You wanna' drink?

(AUSTIN *offers bottle to* LEE, LEE *takes it, sits down on kitchen floor with* AUSTIN, *they share the bottle.*)

Yeah, he lost his real teeth one at a time. Woke up every morning with another tooth lying on the mattress. Finally, he decides he's gotta' get 'em all pulled out but he doesn't have any money. Middle of Arizona with no money and no insurance and every morning another tooth is lying on the mattress. (*Takes a drink.*) So what does he do?

LEE: I dunno'. I never knew about that.

AUSTIN: He begs the government. GI Bill or some damn thing. Some pension plan he remembers in the back of his head. And they send him out the money.

LEE: They did?

(*They keep trading the bottle between them, taking drinks.*)

AUSTIN: Yeah. They send him the money but it's not enough money. Costs a lot to have all yer teeth yanked. They charge by the individual tooth, ya' know. I mean one tooth isn't equal to another tooth. Some are more expensive. Like the big ones in the back—

LEE: So what happened?

AUSTIN: So he locates a Mexican dentist in Juarez who'll do the whole thing for a song. And he takes off hitchhiking to the border.

LEE: Hitchhiking?

AUSTIN: Yeah. So how long you think it takes him to get to the border? A man his age.

LEE: I dunno'.

AUSTIN: Eight days it takes him. Eight days in the rain and the sun and every

to confide in *G.* sich jdm. anvertrauen **mattress** *G.* Matratze **insurance** *G.* Versicherung **GI Bill** a bill that helped veterans financially after World War II **pension** *G.* Rente **to trade** to pass backwards and forwards **to yank** to pull out with a sharp, sudden movement **to locate** to find **for a song** ● for almost nothing **to hitchhike** to travel by asking for rides from motorists along the way

day he's droppin' teeth on the blacktop and nobody'll pick him up 'cause his mouth's full 'a blood.

(Pause, they drink.)

So finally he stumbles into the dentist. Dentist takes all his money and all his teeth. And there he is, in Mexico, with his gums sewed up and his pockets empty.

(Long silence, AUSTIN *drinks.)*

LEE: That's it?

AUSTIN: Then I go out to see him, see. I go out there and I take him out for a nice Chinese dinner. But he doesn't eat. All he wants to do is drink Martinis outa' plastic cups. And he takes his teeth out and lays 'em on the table 'cause he can't stand the feel of 'em. And we ask the waitress for one a' those doggie bags to take the Chop Suey home in. So he drops his teeth in the doggie bag along with the Chop Suey. And then we go out to hit all the bars up and down the highway. Says he wants to introduce me to all his buddies. And in one a' those bars, in one a' those bars up and down the highway, he left that doggie bag with his teeth lying in the Chop Suey.

LEE: You never found it?

AUSTIN: We went back but we never did find it. *(Pause)* Now that's a true story. True to life.

(They drink as lights fade to black.)

Scene Eight

Very early morning, between night and day, no crickets, coyotes yapping feverishly in distance before light comes up. A small fire blazes up in the dark from alcove area, sound of LEE *smashing typewriter with a golf club, lights coming up,* LEE *seen smashing typewriter methodically then dropping pages of his script into a burning bowl set on the floor of alcove, flames leap up.* AUSTIN *has a whole bunch of stolen toasters lined up on the sink counter along with Lee's stolen TV. The toasters are of a wide variety of models, mostly chrome,* AUSTIN *goes up and down the line of toasters, breathing on them and polishing them with a dish towel. Both men are drunk, empty whiskey bottles and beer*

blacktop *A.E.* top asphalt layer of a road **to stumble** to walk unsteadily almost falling over **gums** *G.* Zahnfleisch **gums sewed up** *here:* the drawn-in look of the mouth when the teeth have been taken out **doggie bag** *A.E.* bag supplied by restaurants for taking food home (originally for pets) **Chop Suey** [ˌtʃɒp ˈsuːɪ] Chinese-type meal **to hit the bars** ● to go from one bar to another **a fire blazes** *G.* das Feuer brennt lichterloh **flames leap up** *G.* aufflammen

cans litter floor of kitchen, they share a half-empty bottle on one of the chairs in the alcove, LEE *keeps periodically taking deliberate ax-chops at the typewriter, using a nine-iron as* AUSTIN *speaks, all of their mother's house plants are dead and drooping.*

AUSTIN: (*Polishing toasters*) There's gonna' be a general lack of toast in the neighborhood this morning. Many, many unhappy, bewildered breakfast faces. I guess it's best not to even think of the victims. Not to even entertain it. Is that the right psychology?

LEE: (*Pauses*) What?

AUSTIN: Is that the correct criminal psychology? Not to think of the victims?

LEE: What victims? (*He takes another swipe at typewriter with nine-iron, adds pages to the fire.*)

AUSTIN: The victims of crime. Of breaking and entering. I mean is it a prerequisite for a criminal not to have a conscience?

LEE: Ask a criminal (*Pause.* LEE *stares at* AUSTIN.) What're you gonna' do with all those toasters? That's the dumbest thing I ever saw in my life.

AUSTIN: I've got hundreds of dollars' worth of household appliances here. You may not realize that.

LEE: Yeah, and how many hundreds of dollars did you walk right past?

AUSTIN: It was toasters you challenged me to. Only toasters. I ignored every other temptation.

LEE: I never challenged you! That's no challenge. Anybody can steal a toaster. (*He smashes typewriter again.*)

AUSTIN: You don't have to take it out on my typewriter ya' know. It's not the machine's fault that you can't write. It's a sin to do that to a good machine.

LEE: A sin?

AUSTIN: When you consider all the writers who never even had a machine. Who would have given an eyeball for a good typewriter. Any typewriter. (LEE *smashes typewriter again.*)
(*Polishing toasters.*) All the ones who wrote on matchbook covers. Paper bags. Toilet paper. Who had their writing destroyed by their jailers. Who persisted beyond all odds. Those writers would find it hard to understand your actions.

(LEE *comes down on typewriter with one final crushing blow of the nine-iron then collapses in one of the chairs, takes a drink from bottle. Pause*)

to litter to leave things lying around untidily **to take ax(e)-chops** to hit hard on s.th. as if using an axe **nine iron** type of golf club **to droop** to hang down **bewildered** *G.* bestürzt **to swipe** to hit wildly **prerequisite** [ˌpriːˈrekwɪzɪt] *G.* Vorbedingung **conscience** *G.* Gewissen **to challenge s.o. to do s.th.** *G.* auffordern **temptation** *G.* Versuchung **sin** s.th. against moral law **eyeball** eye **jailers** officers in charge of prisoners **to persist** to continue doing s.th. **odds** factors against

(*After pause.*) Not to mention demolishing a perfectly good golf club. What about all the struggling golfers? What about Lee Trevino? What do you think he would've said when he was batting balls around with broom sticks at the age of nine. Impoverished.

(*Pause*)

LEE: What time is it anyway?

AUSTIN: No idea. Time stands still when you're havin' fun.

LEE: Is it too late to call a woman? You know any women?

AUSTIN: I'm a married man.

LEE: I mean a local woman.

(AUSTIN *looks out at light through window above sink.*)

AUSTIN: It's either too late or too early. You're the nature enthusiast. Can't you tell the time by the light in the sky? Orient yourself around the North Star or something?

LEE: I can't tell anything.

AUSTIN: Maybe you need a little breakfast. Some toast! How 'bout some toast?

(AUSTIN *goes to cupboard, pulls out loaf of bread and starts dropping slices into every toaster,* LEE *stays sitting, drinks, watches* AUSTIN.)

LEE: I don't need toast. I need a woman.

AUSTIN: A woman isn't the answer. Never was.

LEE: I'm not talkin' about permanent. I'm talkin' about temporary.

AUSTIN: (*Putting toast in toasters*) We'll just test the merits of these little demons. See which brands have a tendency to burn. See which one can produce a perfectly golden piece of fluffy toast.

LEE: How much gas you got in yer car?

AUSTIN: I haven't driven my car for days now. So I haven't had an opportunity to look at the gas gauge.

LEE: Take a guess. You think there's enough to get me to Bakersfield?

AUSTIN: Bakersfield? What's in Bakersfield?

LEE: Just never mind what's in Bakersfield! You think there's enough goddamn gas in the car!

AUSTIN: Sure.

LEE: Sure. You could care less, right. Let me run outa' gas on the Grapevine. You could give a shit.

Lee Trevino well-known professional golfer **to bat** to hit **broom stick** *G.* Besenstiel **impoverished** [ɪm'pɒvərɪʃt] made poor **local** from nearby **how about** *G.* wie wäre es **merit** worth, value **brand** manufacturer's name for a product **to have a tendency** *G.* dazu neigen **fluffy** soft and light **gas gauge** [geɪdʒ] *G.* Tankanzeiger; shows how much gas you have in your tank **Bakersfield** city in North California **Grapevine** name of a road

AUSTIN: I'd say there was enough gas to get you just about anywhere, Lee. With your determination and guts.

LEE: What the hell time is it anyway?

(LEE *pulls out his wallet, starts going through dozens of small pieces of paper, with phone numbers written on them, drops some on the floor, drops others in the fire.*)

AUSTIN: Very early. This is the time of morning when the coyotes kill people's cocker spaniels. Did you hear them? That's what they were doing out there. Luring innocent pets away from their homes.

LEE: (*Searching through his papers*) What's the area code for Bakersfield? You know?

AUSTIN: You could always call the operator.

LEE: I can't stand that voice they give ya'.

AUSTIN: What voice?

LEE: That voice that warns you that if you'd only tried harder to find the number in the phone book you wouldn't have to be calling the operator to begin with. (*He gets up, holding a slip of paper from his wallet, stumbles toward phone on wall, yanks receiver, starts dialing.*)

AUSTIN: Well I don't understand why you'd want to talk to anybody else anyway. I mean you can talk to me. I'm your brother.

LEE: (*Dialing*) I wanna' talk to a woman. I haven't heard a woman's voice in a long time.

AUSTIN: Not since the Botanist?

LEE: What?

AUSTIN: Nothing. (*Starts singing as he tends toast.*)

Red sails in the sunset
Way out on the blue
Please carry me loved one
Home safely to me.

LEE: Hey, knock it off will ya'! This is long distance here.

AUSTIN: Bakersfield?

LEE: Yeah, Bakersfield. It's Kern County.

AUSTIN: Well, what County are *we* in?

LEE: You better get yourself a 7-Up, boy.

AUSTIN: One County's as good as another.

(AUSTIN *hums "Red Sails" softly as* LEE *talks on phone.*)

guts △ courage **wallet** small, flat case for holding paper money **to lure** to attract with an intention of harming **I can't stand it** ● I dislike it **slip** small piece of paper **to yank** [jæŋk] ● to pull away with force **to tend** to watch over **knock it off** △ stop it **long distance** *A.E.* Ferngespräch **Kern** a river in south central California **7-Up** lemonade drink

LEE: (*To phone*) Yeah, operator, look—first off I wanna' know the area code for Bakersfield. Right. Bakersfield! Okay. Good. Now I wanna' know if you can help me track somebody down. (*Pause*) No, no I mean a phone number. Just a phone number. Okay. (*Holds piece of paper up and reads it.*) Okay, the name is Melly Ferguson. Melly. (*Pause*) I dunno'. Melly. Maybe. Yeah. Maybe Melanie. Yeah. Melanie Ferguson. Okay. (*Pause*) What? I can't hear ya' so good. Sounds like yer under the ocean. (*Pause*) You got ten Melanie Fergusons? How could that be? Ten Melanie Fergusons in Bakersfield? Well gimme all of 'em then. (*Pause*) What d'ya' mean? Gimme all ten Melanie Fergusons! That's right. Just a second. (*To* AUSTIN.) Gimme a pen.

AUSTIN: I don't have a pen.

LEE: Gimme a pencil then!

AUSTIN: I don't have a pencil.

LEE: (*To phone*) Just a second, operator. (*To* AUSTIN.) Yer a writer and ya' don't have a pen or a pencil!

AUSTIN: I'm not a writer. You're a writer.

LEE: I'm on the phone here! Get me a pen or a pencil.

AUSTIN: I gotta' watch the toast.

LEE: (*To phone*) Hang on a second, operator.

(LEE *lets the phone drop then starts pulling all the drawers in the kitchen out on the floor and dumping the contents, searching for a pencil,* AUSTIN *watches him casually.*)

(*Crashing through drawers, throwing contents around kitchen.*) This is the last time I try to live with people, boy! I can't believe it. Here I am! Here I am again in a desperate situation! This would never happen out on the desert. I would never be in this kinda' situation out on the desert. Isn't there a pen or pencil in this house! Who lives in this house anyway!

AUSTIN: Our mother.

LEE: How come she don't have a pen or a pencil! She's a social person isn't she? Doesn't she have to make shopping lists? She's gotta' have a pencil. (*Finds a pencil.*) Aaha! (*He rushes back to phone, picks up receiver.*) All right, operator. Operator? Hey! Operator! Goddamnit! (*He rips the phone off the wall and throws it down, goes back to chair and falls into it, drinks. Long pause.*)

AUSTIN: She hung up?

LEE: Yeah, she hung up. I knew she was gonna' hang up. I could hear it in her voice. (*He starts going through his slips of paper again.*)

to track s.o. down ● to find s.o. **hang on** ● wait a moment **to dump** to put down carelessly **desperate** ['despərət] almost impossible **how come?** ● *A.E.* why? **to rip** to pull roughly **to hang up** to cut short a telephone call

AUSTIN: Well, you're probably better off staying here with me anyway. I'll take care of you.

LEE: I don't need takin' care of! Not by you anyway.

AUSTIN: Toast is almost ready. (*He starts buttering all the toast as it pops up.*)

LEE: I don't want any toast!

(*Long pause.*)

AUSTIN: You gotta' eat something. Can't just drink. How long have we been drinking, anyway?

LEE: (*Looking through slips of paper*) Maybe it was Fresno. What's the area code for Fresno? How could I have lost that number! She was beautiful.

(*Pause*)

AUSTIN: Why don't you just forget about that, Lee. Forget about the woman.

LEE: She had green eyes. You know what green eyes do to me?

AUSTIN: I know but you're not gonna' get it on with her now anyway. It's dawn already. She's in Bakersfield for Christ's sake.

(*Long pause,* LEE *considers the situation.*)

LEE: Yeah. (*Looks at windows.*) It's dawn!

AUSTIN: Let's just have some toast and—

LEE: What is this bullshit with the toast anyway! You make it sound like salvation or something. I don't want any goddamn toast! How many times I gotta' tell ya'!

(LEE *gets up, crosses up stage to windows in alcove, looks out.* AUSTIN *butters toast.*)

AUSTIN: Well it is like salvation sort of. I mean the smell. I love the smell of toast. And the sun's coming up. It makes me feel like anything's possible. Ya' know?

LEE: (*Back to* AUSTIN, *facing windows up stage*) So go to church why don't ya'.

AUSTIN: Like a beginning. I love beginnings.

LEE: Oh yeah. I've always been kinda' partial to endings myself.

AUSTIN: What if I come with you, Lee?

LEE: (*Pause as* LEE *turns toward* AUSTIN) What?

AUSTIN: What if I come with you out to the desert?

LEE: Are you kiddin'?

AUSTIN: No. I'd just like to see what it's like.

LEE: You wouldn't last a day out there pal.

AUSTIN: That's what you said about the toasters. You said I couldn't steal a toaster either.

LEE: A toaster's got nothin' to do with the desert.

Fresno city in California **dawn** beginning of the day **salvation** rescue or forgiveness from sin **partial to** ● to have a liking for **pal** ● good friend

AUSTIN: I could make it, Lee. I'm not that helpless. I can cook.

LEE: Cook?

AUSTIN: I can.

LEE: So what! You can cook. Toast.

AUSTIN: I can make fires. I know how to get fresh water from condensation. (AUSTIN *stacks buttered toast up in a tall stack on plate.* LEE *slams table.*)

LEE: It's not somethin' you learn out of a Boy Scout Handbook!

AUSTIN: Well how do you learn it then! How're you supposed to learn it! (*Pause*)

LEE: Ya' just learn it, that's all. Ya' learn it 'cause ya' have to learn it. You don't *have* to learn it.

AUSTIN: You could teach me.

LEE: (*Stands*) What're you, crazy or somethin'? You went to college. Here, you are down here, rollin' in bucks. Floatin' up and down in elevators. And you wanna' learn how to live on the desert!

AUSTIN: I do, Lee. I really do. There's nothin' down here for me. There never was. When we were kids here it was different. There was a life here then. But now—I keep comin' down here thinkin' it's the fifties or somethin'. I keep finding myself getting off the freeway at familiar landmarks that turn out to be unfamiliar. On the way to appointments. Wandering down streets I thought I recognized that turn out to be replicas of streets I remember. Streets I misremember. Streets I can't tell if I lived on or saw in a postcard. Fields that don't even exist anymore.

LEE: There's no point cryin' about that now.

AUSTIN: There's nothin' real down here, Lee! Least of all me!

LEE: Well I can't save you from that!

AUSTIN: You can let me come with you.

LEE: No dice, pal.

AUSTIN: You could let me come with you, Lee!

LEE: Hey, do you actually think I chose to live out in the middle a' nowhere? Do ya'? Ya' think it's some kinda' philosophical decision I took or somethin'? I'm livin' out there 'cause I can't make it here! And yer bitchin' to me about all yer success!

AUSTIN: I'd cash it all in in a second. That's the truth.

LEE: (*Pause, shakes his head*) I can't believe this.

AUSTIN: Let me go with you.

condensation *G.* Kondensation **Boy Scout Handbook** *G.* Pfadfinderfibel **to roll in s.th.** ● to have a lot of **to float up and down (in elevators)** to go up and down (in elevators) **replica** ['replɪkə] imitation, reproduction, copy **misremember** remember incorrectly **no dice** △ *G.* kommt nicht in Frage; no, I'm not doing it, no, you can't do it **to bitch about s.th.** △ *A.E.* to complain

LEE: Stop sayin' that will ya'! Yer worse than a dog.

(AUSTIN *offers out the plate of neatly stacked toast to* LEE.)

AUSTIN: You want some toast?

(LEE *suddenly explodes and knocks the plate out of* AUSTIN'*s hand, toast goes flying. Long frozen moment where it appears* LEE *might go all the way this time when* AUSTIN *breaks it by slowly lowering himself to his knees and begins gathering the scattered toast from the floor and stacking it back on the plate.* LEE *begins to circle* AUSTIN *in a slow, predatory way, crushing pieces of toast in his wake, no words for a while.* AUSTIN *keeps gathering toast, even the crushed pieces.*)

LEE: Tell ya' what I'll do little brother. I might just consider makin' you a deal. Little trade.

(AUSTIN *continues gathering toast as* LEE *circles him through this.*)

You write me up this screenplay thing just like I tell ya'. I mean you can use all yer usual tricks and stuff. Yer fancy language. Yer artistic hocus pocus. But ya' gotta' write everything like I say. Every move. Every time they run outa' gas, they run outa' gas. Every time they wanna' jump on a horse, they do just that. If they wanna' stay in Texas, by God they'll stay in Texas! (*Keeps circling.*) And you finish the whole thing up for me. Top to bottom. And you put my name on it. And I own all the rights. And every dime goes in my pocket. You do all that and I'll sure enough take ya' with me to the desert. (LEE *stops, pause, looks down at* AUSTIN.) How's that sound?

(*Pause as* AUSTIN *stands slowly, holding plate of demolished toast. Their faces are very close, pause.*)

AUSTIN: It's a deal.

(LEE *stares straight into* AUSTIN'*s eyes, then he slowly takes a piece of toast off the plate, raises it to his mouth and takes a huge crushing bite, never taking his eyes off* AUSTIN'*s. As* LEE *crunches into the toast the lights black out.*)

Scene Nine

Mid-day, no sound, blazing heat, the stage is ravaged; bottles, toasters, smashed typewriter, ripped out telephone, etc. All the debris from previous scene is now starkly visible in intense yellow light; the effect should be like a desert junkyard at high noon, the coolness of the preceding scenes is totally

predator ['predətə(r)] animal that lives by killing and feeding off other animals **wake** *here:* trail, behind him **dime** *A.E.* coin worth ten cents **to ravage** ['rævɪdʒ] to destroy violently **debris** ['deɪbri:] *US* [də'bri:] broken pieces left after an explosion **junkyard** place where old metal, furniture etc. are collected and resold

obliterated. AUSTIN *is seated at table in alcove, shirt open, pouring with sweat, hunched over a writing notebook, scribbling notes desperately with a ballpoint pen.* LEE *with no shirt, beer in hand, sweat pouring down his chest, is walking a slow circle around the table, picking his way through the objects, sometimes kicking them aside.*

LEE: (*As he walks*) All right, read it back to me. Read it back to me!

AUSTIN: (*Scribbling at top speed*) Just a second.

LEE: Come on, come on! Just read what ya' got.

AUSTIN: I can't keep up! It's not the same as if I had a typewriter.

LEE: Just read what we got so far. Forget about the rest.

AUSTIN: All right. Let's see—okay—

(AUSTIN *wipes sweat from his face, reads as* LEE *circles.*)

Luke says uh—

LEE: Luke?

AUSTIN: Yeah.

LEE: His name's Luke? All right, all right—we can change the names later. What's he say? Come on, come on.

AUSTIN: He says uh—(*Reading*) "I told ya' you were a fool to follow me in here. I know this prairie like the back a' my hand."

LEE: No, no, no! That's not what I said. I never said that.

AUSTIN: That's what I wrote.

LEE: It's not what I said. I never said "like the back a' my hand". That's stupid. That's one a' those—whadya' call it? Whadya' call that?

AUSTIN: What?

LEE: Whadya' call it when somethin's been said a thousand times before. Whadya' call that?

AUSTIN: Um—a cliché?

LEE: Yeah. That's right. Cliché. That's what that is. A cliché. "The back a' my hand." That's stupid.

AUSTIN: That's what you said.

LEE: I never said that! And even if I did, that's where yer supposed to come in. That's where yer supposed to change it to somethin' better.

AUSTIN: Well how am I supposed to do that and write down what you say at the same time?

LEE: Ya' just do, that's all! You hear a stupid line you change it. That's yer job.

AUSTIN: All right. (*Makes more notes.*)

LEE: What're you changin' it to?

to obliterate [ə'blɪtəreɪt] to wipe out, erase **to scribble** to write quickly and untidily **ballpoint pen** *G.* Kugelschreiber **to know s.th. like the back of one's hand** to know s.th. extremely well

AUSTIN: I'm not changing it. I'm just trying to catch up.

LEE: Well change it! We gotta' change that, we can't leave that in there like that. "... the back a' my hand." That's dumb.

AUSTIN: (*Stops writing, sits back*) All right.

LEE: (*Pacing*) So what'll we change it to?

AUSTIN: Um—How 'bout—"I'm on intimate terms with this prairie."

LEE: (*To himself, considering line as he walks*) "I'm on intimate terms with this prairie." Intimate terms, intimate terms. Intimate—that means like uh—sexual, right?

AUSTIN: Well—yeah—or—

LEE: He's on sexual terms with the prairie? How dya' figure that?

AUSTIN: Well it doesn't necessarily have to mean sexual.

LEE: What's it mean then?

AUSTIN: It means uh—close—personal—

LEE: All right. How's it sound? Put it into the uh—the line there. Read it back. Let's see how it sounds. (*To himself.*) "Intimate terms."

AUSTIN: (*Scribbles in notebook*) Okay. It'd go something like this: (*Reads*) "I told ya' you were a fool to follow me in here. I'm on intimate terms with this prairie."

LEE: That's good. I like that. That's real good.

AUSTIN: You do?

LEE: Yeah. Don't you?

AUSTIN: Sure.

LEE: Sounds original now. "Intimate terms." That's good. Okay. Now we're cookin'! That has a real ring to it.

(AUSTIN *makes more notes,* LEE *walks around, pours beer on his arms and rubs it over his chest feeling good about the new progress. As he does this* MOM *enters unobtrusively down stage left with her luggage. She stops and stares at the scene, still holding luggage, as the two men continue, unaware of her presence,* AUSTIN *absorbed in his writing,* LEE *cooling himself off with beer.* LEE *continues.*)

"He's on intimate terms with this prairie." Sounds real mysterious and kinda' threatening at the same time.

AUSTIN: (*Writing rapidly*) Good.

LEE: Now—

(LEE *turns and suddenly sees* MOM, *he stares at her for a while, she stares back,* AUSTIN *keeps writing feverishly, not noticing.* LEE *walks slowly over to* MOM *and takes a closer look. Long pause.*)

terms *G.* Beziehung **we're cookin'** △ *A.E., G. etwa:* jetzt sind wir in Fahrt **ring** resonance **unobtrusive** [ˌʌnəbˈtruːsɪv] not noticed

Mom?

(AUSTIN *looks up suddenly from his writing, sees* MOM, *stands quickly, long pause.* MOM *surveys the damage.*)

AUSTIN: Mom. What're you doing back?

MOM: I'm back.

LEE: Here, lemme take those for ya'.

(LEE *sets beer on counter then takes both her bags, but doesn't know where to set them down in the sea of junk so he just keeps holding them.*)

AUSTIN: I wasn't expecting you back so soon. I thought uh—How was Alaska?

MOM: Fine.

LEE: See any igloos?

MOM: No. Just glaciers.

AUSTIN: Cold, huh?

MOM: What?

AUSTIN: It must've been cold up there?

MOM: Not really.

LEE: Musta' been colder than this here. I mean we're havin' a real scorcher here.

MOM: Oh? (*She looks at damage.*)

LEE: Yeah. Must be in the hundreds.

AUSTIN: You wanna' take your coat off, Mom?

MOM: No. (*Pause, she surveys space.*) What happened in here?

AUSTIN: Oh um—Me and Lee were just sort of celebrating and uh—

MOM: Celebrating?

AUSTIN: Yeah. Uh—Lee sold a screenplay. A story, I mean.

MOM: Lee did?

AUSTIN: Yeah.

MOM: Not you?

AUSTIN: No. Him.

MOM: (*To* LEE) You sold a screenplay?

LEE: Yeah. That's right. We're just sorta' finishing it up right now. That's what we're doing here.

AUSTIN: Me and Lee are going out to the desert to live.

MOM: You and Lee?

AUSTIN: Yeah. I'm taking off with Lee.

MOM: (*She looks back and forth at each of them. Pause*) You gonna' go live with your father?

glacier ['glæsjə(r)] mass of ice moving slowly down a valley **scorcher** ● exceptionally hot day **to scorch** to burn slightly **in the hundreds** over 100 degrees Fahrenheit **to take off** ● to go away leaving everything behind

AUSTIN: No. We're going to a different desert, Mom.

MOM: I see. Well, you'll probably wind up on the same desert sooner or later. What're all these toasters doing here?

AUSTIN: Well—we had a kind of contest.

MOM: Contest?

LEE: Yeah.

AUSTIN: Lee won.

MOM: Did you win a lot of money, Lee?

LEE: Well, not yet. It's comin' in any day now.

MOM: (*To* LEE) What happened to your shirt?

LEE: Oh. I was sweatin' like a pig and I took it off.

(AUSTIN *grabs* LEE'*s shirt off the table and tosses it to him.* LEE *sets down suitcases and puts his shirt on.*)

MOM: Well it's one hell of a mess in here isn't it?

AUSTIN: Yeah, I'll clean it up for you, Mom. I just didn't know you were coming back so soon.

to wind up ● to finish, find oneself in a certain situation **contest** competition **mess** *G.* Durcheinander

MOM: I didn't either.

AUSTIN: What happened?

MOM: Nothing. I just started missing all my plants. (*She notices dead plants.*)

AUSTIN: Oh.

MOM: Oh, they're all dead aren't they. (*She crosses toward them, examines them closely.*) You didn't get a chance to water, I guess.

AUSTIN: I was doing it and then Lee came and—

LEE: Yeah I just distracted him a whole lot here, Mom. It's not his fault.

(*Pause, as* MOM *stares at plants.*)

MOM: Oh well, one less thing to take care of I guess. (*Turns toward brothers.*) Oh, that reminds me—You boys will probably never guess who's in town. Try and guess.

(*Long pause, brothers stare at her.*)

AUSTIN: Whadya' mean, Mom?

MOM: Take a guess. Somebody very important has come to town. I read it, coming down on the Greyhound.

LEE: Somebody very important?

MOM: See if you can guess. You'll never guess.

AUSTIN: Mom—we're trying to uh—(*Points to writing pad.*)

MOM: Picasso. (*Pause*) Picasso's in town. Isn't that incredible? Right now.

(*Pause*)

AUSTIN: Picasso's dead, Mom.

MOM: No, he's not dead. He's visiting the museum. I read it on the bus. We have to go down there and see him.

AUSTIN: Mom—

MOM: This is the chance of a lifetime. Can you imagine? We could all go down and meet him. All three of us.

LEE: Uh—I don't think I'm really up fer meetin' anybody right now. I'm uh—What's his name?

MOM: Picasso! Picasso! You've never heard of Picasso? Austin, you've heard of Picasso.

AUSTIN: Mom, we're not going to have time.

MOM: It won't take long. We'll just hop in the car and go down there. An opportunity like this doesn't come along every day.

AUSTIN: We're gonna' be leavin' here, Mom!

(*Pause*)

MOM: Oh.

to distract to draw s.o.'s attention away from s.th. **Greyhound** *A.E.* famous transcontinental bus line in the USA **Picasso** famous modern painter **to be up for/to s.th.** ● to feel like doing s.th. **to hop in the car** ● to get into the car quickly

LEE: Yeah.

(*Pause*)

MOM: You're both leaving?

LEE: (*Looks at* AUSTIN) Well we were thinkin' about that before but now I—

AUSTIN: No, we are! We're both leaving. We've got it all planned.

MOM: (*To* AUSTIN) Well you can't leave. You have a family.

AUSTIN: I'm leaving. I'm getting out of here.

LEE: (*To* MOM) I don't really think Austin's cut out for the desert, do you?

MOM: No. He's not.

AUSTIN: I'm going with you, Lee!

MOM: He's too thin.

LEE: Yeah, he'd just burn up out there.

AUSTIN: (*To* LEE) We just gotta' finish this screenplay and then we're gonna' take off. That's the plan. That's what you said. Come on, let's get back to work, Lee.

LEE: I can't work under these conditions here. It's too hot.

AUSTIN: Then we'll do it on the desert.

LEE: Don't be tellin' me what we're gonna' do!

MOM: Don't shout in the house.

LEE: We're just gonna' have to postpone the whole deal.

AUSTIN: I can't postpone it! It's gone past postponing! I'm doing everything you said. I'm writing down exactly what you tell me.

LEE: Yeah, but you were right all along see. It is a dumb story. "Two lame-brains chasin' each other across Texas." That's what you said, right?

AUSTIN: I never said that.

(LEE *sneers in* AUSTIN'*s face, then turns to* MOM.)

LEE: I'm gonna' just borrow some a' your antiques, Mom. You don't mind do ya'? Just a few plates and things. Silverware.

(LEE *starts going through all the cupboards in the kitchen, pulling out plates and stacking them on counter as* MOM *and* AUSTIN *watch.*)

MOM: You don't have any utensils on the desert?

LEE: Nah, I'm fresh out.

AUSTIN: (*To* LEE) What're you doing?

MOM: Well some of those are very old. Bone china.

LEE: I'm tired of eatin' outa' my bare hands, ya' know. It's not civilized.

AUSTIN: (*To* LEE) What're you doing? We made a deal!

he isn't cut out for the desert ['dezət] ● he doesn't have any interest in it, he doesn't have the talent to do it **to burn up** ● *A.E.* to lose all interest in everything **to postpone** to do s.th. later than planned **to sneer** to smile contemptuously **I'm fresh out of s.th.** ● I have just used up the last I had **bone china** fine porcelain made of white clay, bone ash or calcium phosphate

MOM: Couldn't you borrow the plastic ones instead? I have plenty of plastic ones.

LEE: (*As he stacks plates*) It's not the same. Plastic's not the same at all. What I need it somethin' authentic. Somethin' to keep me in touch. It's easy to get outa' touch out there. Don't worry I'll get 'em back to ya'.

(AUSTIN *rushes up to* LEE, *grabs him by shoulders.*)

AUSTIN: You can't just drop the whole thing, Lee!

(LEE *turns, pushes* AUSTIN *in the chest, knocking him backwards into the alcove.* MOM *watches numbly,* LEE *returns to collecting the plates, silverware, etc.*)

MOM: You boys shouldn't fight in the house. Go outside and fight.

LEE: I'm not fightin'. I'm leavin'.

MOM: There's been enough damage done already.

LEE: (*His back to* AUSTIN *and* MOM, *stacking dishes on counter*) I'm clearin' outa' here once and for all. All this town does is drive a man insane. Look what it's done to Austin there. I'm not lettin' that happen to me. Sell myself down the river. No sir. I'd rather be a hundred miles from nowhere than let that happen to me.

(*During this,* AUSTIN *has picked up the ripped-out phone from the floor and wrapped the cord tightly around both his hands. He lunges at* LEE *whose back is still to him, wraps the cord around* LEE'*s neck, plants a foot in* LEE'*s back and pulls back on the cord, tightening it.* LEE *chokes desperately, can't speak and can't reach* AUSTIN *with his arms.* AUSTIN *keeps applying pressure on* LEE'*s back with his foot, bending him into the sink.* MOM *watches.*)

AUSTIN: (*Tightening cord*) You're not goin' anywhere! You're not takin' anything with you. You're not takin' my car! You're not takin' the dishes! You're not takin' anything! You're stayin' right here!

MOM: You'll have to stop fighting in the house. There's plenty of room outside to fight. You've got the whole outdoors to fight in.

(LEE *tries to tear himself away. He crashes across the stage like an enraged bull, dragging* AUSTIN *with him. He snorts and bellows but* AUSTIN *hangs on and manages to keep clear of* LEE'*s attempts to grab him. They crash into the table, to the floor.* LEE *is face down thrashing wildly and choking,* AUSTIN *pulls cord tighter, stands with one foot planted on* LEE'*s back and the cord stretched taut.*)

to keep in touch/to be out of touch to be in/out of contact **numb** [nʌm] with no feeling **damage** *G.* Schaden **once and for all** for ever **insane** [ɪn'seɪn] mentally ill **to sell s.o. down the river** ● to betray s.o. **to choke** [tʃəʊk] to be unable to breathe because of s.th. in the throat **enraged** wildly angry **to snort** *G.* schnauben **to thrash** to move the arms and legs about violently **taut** [tɔːt] very tight

AUSTIN: (*Holding cord*) Gimme back my keys, Lee! Take the keys out! Take 'em out!

(LEE *desperately tries to dig in his pockets, searching for the car keys.* MOM *moves closer.*)

MOM: (*Calmly to* AUSTIN) You're not killing him are you?

AUSTIN: I don't know. I don't know if I'm killing him. I'm stopping him. That's all. I'm just stopping him.

(LEE *thrashes but* AUSTIN *is relentless.*)

MOM: You oughta' let him breathe a little bit.

AUSTIN: Throw the keys out, Lee!

(LEE *finally gets keys out and throws them on floor but out of* AUSTIN*'s reach.* AUSTIN *keeps pressure on cord, pulling* LEE*'s neck back.* LEE *gets one hand to the cord but can't relieve the pressure.*)

Reach me those keys would ya', Mom?

MOM: (*Not moving*) Why are you doing this to him?

AUSTIN: Reach me the keys!

relentless [rɪ'lentles] without pity

MOM: Not until you stop choking him.

AUSTIN: I can't stop choking him! He'll kill me if I stop choking him!

MOM: He won't kill you. He's your brother.

AUSTIN: Just get me the keys would ya'!

(Pause. MOM *picks keys off floor, hands them to* AUSTIN.)

(To MOM.) Thanks.

MOM: Will you let him go now?

AUSTIN: I don't know. He's not gonna' let me get outa' here.

MOM: Well you can't kill him.

AUSTIN: I can kill him! I can easily kill him. Right now. Right here. All I gotta' do is just tighten up. See?

(AUSTIN *tightens cord,* LEE *thrashes wildly,* AUSTIN *releases pressure a little, maintaining control.*)

Ya' see that?

MOM: That's a savage thing to do.

AUSTIN: Yeah well don't tell me I can't kill him, because I can. I can just twist. I can keep twisting.

(AUSTIN *twists the cord tighter,* LEE *weakens, his breathing changes to a short rasp.*)

MOM: Austin!

(AUSTIN *relieves pressure,* LEE *breathes easier but* AUSTIN *keeps him under control.*)

AUSTIN: (*Eyes on* LEE, *holding cord*) I'm goin' to the desert. There's nothing stopping me. I'm going by myself to the desert.

MOM: (*Moving toward her luggage*) Well, I'm going to go check into a motel. I can't stand this anymore.

AUSTIN: Don't go yet!

(MOM *pauses.*)

MOM: I can't stay here. This is worse than being homeless.

AUSTIN: I'll get everything fixed up for you, Mom. I promise. Just stay for a while.

MOM: (*Picking up luggage*) You're going to the desert.

AUSTIN: Just wait!

(LEE *thrashes,* AUSTIN *subdues him,* MOM *watches, holding luggage. Pause*)

MOM: It was the worst feeling being up there. In Alaska. Staring out a window. I never felt so desperate before. That's why when I saw that article on Picasso I thought—

AUSTIN: Stay here, Mom. This is where you live.

savage cruel, brutal **rasp** a noise associated with gasping for breath **to subdue s.o.** to keep or put s.o. under control **desperation** hopeless despair

(MOM *looks around the stage.*)

MOM: I don't recognize it at all.

(MOM *exits with luggage,* AUSTIN *makes a move toward her but* LEE *starts to struggle and* AUSTIN *subdues him again with cord. Pause*)

AUSTIN: (*Holding cord*) Lee? I'll make ya' a deal. You let me get outa' here. Just let me get to my car. All right, Lee? Gimme a little headstart and I'll turn you loose. Just gimme a little headstart. All right?

(LEE *makes no response,* AUSTIN *slowly releases tension on cord, still nothing from* LEE.)

Lee?

(LEE *is motionless,* AUSTIN *very slowly begins to stand, still keeping a tenuous hold on the cord and his eyes riveted to* LEE *for any sign of movement.* AUSTIN *slowly drops the cord and stands, he stares down at* LEE *who appears to be dead.*)

(*Whispers*) Lee?

(*Pause.* AUSTIN *considers, looks toward exit, back to* LEE, *then makes a small movement as if to leave. Instantly* LEE *is on his feet and moves toward exit, blocking* AUSTIN*'s escape. They square off to each other, keeping a distance between them. Pause. A single coyote heard in distance, lights fade softly into moonlight, the figures of the brothers now appear to be caught in a vast desert-like landscape. They are very still but watchful for the next move. Lights go slowly to black as the after-image of the brothers pulses in the dark, coyote fades.*)

headstart advantage, *here:* time to start in advance **to turn s.o. loose** to free s.o. **tenuous** ['tenjʊəs] *here:* careful **to rivet** ['rɪvɪt] to fix firmly **to square off** ● to stand firmly opposite s.o. waiting for an attack **after-image** image which remains after the stimulus has been removed **to pulse** *G.* pulsieren

Additional Material

1. Productions of *True West*

How the Americans see it

True West San Francisco, July 18.

Magic Theatre presentation of a play in two acts by Sam Shepard; staged by Robert Woodruff; scenery: Jesse Hollis; costumes: Rita Yovino; lighting: Kurt Landisman; sound: Rob Welles. Opened July 11, '80, at the Magic Theatre, San Francisco; 6 top.

Austin	Peter Coyote
Lee	Jim Haynie
Saul Kimmer	Tom Dahlgren
Mom	Carol McElheney

The 99-seat Magic Theatre has been a large launching pad for the remarkably prolific Sam Shepard, whose Pulitzer-winner of 1979, "Buried Child", also preemed in the house, a former Army barracks. Robert Woodruff also staged "Child" and Shepard's "Suicide in B-Flat" here.

The Magic has an Equity waiver, and only one of the four performers in this newest Shepard tale of success-failure and the American Dream reveals a sense of skill and depth. But the play itself is clearly estimable, and fortunately the showiest character, a ne'er-do-well burglar who smells success as a screenwriter, is in the competent hands of Jim Haynie.

The piece is softest in its final few scenes, as Shepard almost gropes toward the inevitable yet reasonable conclusion. The playwright has often been rapped for lacking plot discipline, but all he lacks with "True West" is a

to stage to produce a play in the theatre **launching pad** [lɔːntʃɪn] *G.* Abschußrampe **prolific** (writer) [prəʊ'lɪfɪk] s.o. who writes a lot **preemed** [priːmd] *A.E.* to give a first performance **B-flat** *G.* b-moll **Equity** theatre trade union **to waive** [weɪv] (legal) to say one will not insist on a right or claim **waiver** legal document waiving a right **Equity waiver** the union has agreed to let non-union members act in the play **to reveal** to show, slowly uncover **estimable** ['estɪməbl] praiseworthy **showy** attracting attention **ne'er-do-well** *G.* Taugenichts **burglar** s.o. who breaks into houses and steals **to grope** to search as in the dark **inevitable** [ɪn'evɪtəbl] certain to happen **to rap s.o. for s.th.** ● to criticize severely **to lack s.th.** not have s.th., be without s.th.

stopwatch near the end. Otherwise, the development of the yarn and the two principal characters as brothers couldn't be much more clearly wrought.

Peter Coyote, one-time chairman of Governor Jerry Brown's California Arts Council, is uncomfortably mannered as the screen-writer-brother. He finds himself stuck in his mother's house with his sibling who has broken into so many homes he appears to be acutely disturbed himself.

There's a role reversal, written with fine ironic humor and insight. The highest moment of comedy, skillfully set up by Shepard, comes when the writer turns into a toaster thief and demonstrates his hot goods in a drunken moment. Ultimately the brothers revert to form after leaving their mother's house in a mess, but with their own lives in what passes for order.—Herb.

From: *Variety*, Juli 23, 1980.

yarn story, usually about an adventure, which is difficult to believe **clearly wrought** [rɔːt] *G.* genau dargestellt **uncomfortably mannered** *G.* fühlt sich nicht wohl in seiner Haut **stuck** unable to move away **sibling** brother(s) or sister(s) **hot** △ stolen **to revert** to go back to a former state **mess** *G.* Durcheinander **to pass for s.th.** *G.* gilt als ...

Frank Rich

Shepard's "True West" Myths vs. Reality

Some day, when the warring parties get around to writing their memoirs, we may actually discover who killed "True West", the Sam Shepard play that finally opened at the Public Theater last night. As the press has already reported, this failure is an orphan. Robert Woodruff, the nominal director, left the play in previews and disowned the production. Mr. Shepard has also disowned the production, although he has not ventured from California to see it. The producer Joseph Papp, meanwhile, has been left holding the bag. New Year's will be here shortly, and one can only hope that these talented men will forgive and forget.

At least their battle has been fought for a worthwhile cause. "True West" seems to be a very good Shepard play—which means that it's one of the American theater's most precious natural resources. But no play can hold the stage all by itself. Except for odd moments, when Mr. Shepard's fantastic language rips through the theater on its own sinuous strength, the "True

war *G.* Krieg **to get around to s.th.** finally find time to do s.th. **orphan** child without parents **to disown** to say one no longer wants any connection with s.th. **to venture** to do s.th. which is a risk **worthwhile** *G.* lohnend **odd** single, individual **to rip** *here:* widerhallen, erschallen **sinuous** ['sɪnjʊəs] full of twists and curves

West" at the Public amounts to little more than a stand-up run-through of a text that remains to be explored. This play hasn't been misdirected; it really looks as if it hasn't been directed at all.

You know a play has no director when funny dialogue dies before it reaches the audience. Or when two lead actors step on each other's lines and do "business" rather than create characters. Or when entrances and scene-endings look arbitrary rather than preplanned. Or when big farcical sequences—an avalanche of Coors beer cans, for instance—clatter about the stage creating confusion rather than mirth. Or when an evening's climax—the mystical death embrace of two fratricidal brothers—is so vaguely choreographed it looks like a polka. All these things and more happen at the Public.

It's a terrible shame. "True West" is a worthy direct descendant of Mr. Shepard's "Curse of the Starving Class" and "Buried Child". Many of his persistent recent themes are present and accounted for—the spiritual death of the American family, the corruption of the artist by business, the vanishing of the Western wilderness and its promised dream of freedom. If the playwright dramatizes his concerns in fantastic flights of poetic imagery, that imagery always springs directly from the life of the people and drama he has invented. Mr. Shepard doesn't graft symbols onto his plays. He's a true artist; his best works are organic creations that cannot be broken down into their constituent parts.

The brothers of "True West" are both hustlers, of, if you will, modernday cowboys who have lost their range. Lee (Peter Boyle) is a drifter and petty burglar, and the younger Austin (Tommy Lee Jones) is a screenwriter. The play is about what happens when the two men reunite in their mother's ticky-tacky suburban Los Angeles home. By the end of the evening, they have stolen each other's identities and destroyed the house, and yet they can never completely sever the ties that bind. Like the heroes in the "true life" Hollywood movie western they write during the course of the play, Lee and Austin are "two lamebrains" doomed to chase each other eternally across a desolate, ever-receding frontier.

Mr. Shepard is an awesome writer. When Lee and Austin lament the passing

to amount to add up to **arbitrary** ['a:bɪtrərɪ] *G.* willkürlich **to clatter** *G.* klappern, klirren **mirth** *G.* Heiterkeit **to embrace** to hold s.o. lovingly in one's arms **fratricidal** [ˌfrætrɪsaɪdl] *G.* brudermörderisch **descendant** *G.* Nachkomme **persistent** used again and again **to vanish** to disappear **flight** *here:* Ausbruch, Schwung **to graft s.th. on** einpflanzen **constituent parts** *G.* Bestandteile **range** land on which cowboys work **drifter** *G.* Herumtreiber **petty** small, of little importance **ticky-tacky** ● poorly built **to sever** ['sevə(r)] to cut, separate completely **lamebrain** ● ineffective, useless person **to recede** [rɪ'si:d] *G.* verschwinden, zurückweichen **awe** feeling of respect and fear **to lament** *G.* (be)jammern

of the West they loved (and that maybe never existed), they launch into respectively loopy, nostalgic monologues about the film "Lonely Are the Brave" and the now-extinct neighborhood of their youth. Amusing as they are, these comic riffs are also moving because they give such full life to Mr. Shepard's conflict between America's myths and the bitter, plastic reality that actually exists. Lee can no longer distinguish the true West from the copy he finds in a movie: Austin discovers that his childhood memories are inseparable from the vistas he sees on cheap post cards. Looking for roots, Mr. Shepard's characters fall into a void.

The playwright also provides motifs involving dogs, crickets, desert topography, cars, household appliances (expecially toasters and television sets) and the brothers' unseen, destitute father. As the play progresses, these images keep folding into one another until we are completely transported into the vibrant landscape of Mr. Shepard's imagination. Such is the collective power of this playwright's words that even his wilder conceits seem naturalistic in the context of his play. We never question that Lee would try to destroy a typewriter with a golf club or that the family patriarch would lose his false teeth in a doggie bag full of chop suey.

"True West" slips only when Mr. Shepard, a master of ellipses, tries to fill in his blanks. Does he really need lines like, "There's nothing real here now, least of all me", or, "There's no such thing as the West anymore"? The movie-industry gags, most of which involve a producer in gold chains (Louis Zorich), are jarring as well. Mr. Shepard's witticisms about development deals and agents have been written funnier by Woody Allen and Paul Mazursky, and they bring "True West" down to earth.

Still, these judgments must be tentative. It's impossible to evaluate a play definitively when it hasn't been brought to life on stage. There's nervous energy at the Public, but it leads nowhere. Mr. Boyle, a loping, illshaven figure in baggy clothes, is engagingly sleazy for a while, but his performance trails off into vagueness and repetition just as it should begin to build. Mr. Jones is kinetic and finally frantic as he tries and fails to get a handle on the screenwriter. We never believe that these actors are mirror image brothers locked into a psychological cat-and-mouse game. Theater goers who venture to the Public must depend on their own imagination to supply the crackling timing and the violent tension that are absent.

Who's to blame? Please address your inquiries to the Messrs. Shepard, Woodruff and Papp. And while you're writing, demand restitution. These men owe New York a true "True West".

From: *The New York Times,* December 24, 1980.

to launch into to begin with enthusiasm and energy **loopy** ● crazy **extinct** *G.* ausgestorben **to distinguish** *G.* unterscheiden **void** completely empty space **destitute** ['destɪtjuːt] *G.* mittellos **vibrant** pulsating **conceit** [kən'siːt] *here:* cleverly expressed ideas **blank** empty space **gag** ● joke **to jar** to have an unpleasant effect **tentative** ['tentətɪv] uncertain, weak **to lope** *G.* herumlungern **engaging** charming **sleazy** cheap, poor-looking **to trail off** to become gradually weaker **vague** not clear in shape or form **to get a handle on s.o.** to understand s.o. **crackling** *G.* knisternd **absent** not there, missing **restitution** *G.* Ersatz

How the British see it

Michael Billington

True West

There will doubtless be those who find in Sam Shepard's *True West*, given its British première at the Cottesloe, a piece of pure American poetry. Myself, I think it's thinly-conceived phoney-baloney built according to a stock Shepardian recipe: primal family hatred, reference back to some mythical golden age, a wackily destructive climax. This is underbaked Shepard's pie rather than something hacked out of a genuinely wild, absurdist imagination.

We are in a Californian suburb 40 miles east of LA. Austin, a kempt screenwriter, sits in his mother's kitchen working on a movie interrupted by brother Lee, a rough, hairy man just back from three months in the Mojave desert. And from that point on we witness an ancient fraternal battle. Lee, petty thief and arch-hustler, muscles in on his brother's territory, gets commissioned to write a dud Western and in impotent rage starts tearing the joint apart. Austin's fragile intellectualism meanwhile breaks down as he loses his movie job, gets drunk, rips off all the neighbourhood toasters and starts pining for the desert. By the end, the two brothers are squaring up for a duel-to-the-finish as a coyote barks in the distance.

Obviously Shepard is capitalising on memories of all those American plays (Long Day's Journey, Death of a Salesman) that touch on sibling rivalry. He is

thinly-conceived with weak ideas **phoney-baloney** [bə'ləʊnɪ] *A.E.* unreal nonsense **wackily** in a silly or stupid way **Shepard's pie** shepherd's pie: a hot dish made of minced meat and gravy topped with mashed potatoes **to hack out** ● *G.* behauen **kempt** *G.* gepflegt **arch** first class **hustler** very active person **to muscle in on** ● to use forceful tactics to get what you want **dud** of no use **joint** ● room, building **to rip off** ● to steal **to pine for** to have a strong wish to do s.th. one feels is almost impossible **to square up** to stand opposite to s.o. ready for a fight **to capitalize on** to take advantage of

also suggesting that each brother yearns to have the other's qualities: the doer hungers for a bit of Ivy League class while the thinker pines, more in Thoreau than in anger, for a return to manly primitivism. Each, however, is steeped in illusion just as much as the air-conditioned movie producer who somehow thinks that in the 1980s you can return to the old values of the West and lame-brains chasing each other across the Texan border.

That is the idea. The trouble is that Mr Shepard, at his best a wonderfully instinctive writer with a gift for rhetoric and mad images, is here dryly schematic. You feel that the cool Austin disintegrates to prove a point rather than from internal necessity (in the real world a junked writer would get on to his agent). Equally the anarchic Lee, bashing up a typewriter with a nine-iron symbolises rather than expresses animal power. Even the reduction of the suburban home to chaos doesn't have the recklessness of vintage Shepard: you feel it's there merely to decorate a thesis about American horror at the destruction of the household goods.

In his best plays (Curse of the Starving Class, Buried Child) Mr Shepard gives us detailed family drama going suspiciously awry: here the background is too sketchy to make the descent into the abyss dramatic. There simply aren't enough layers around to be stripped. But in John Schlesinger's atmospheric production there are a couple of extremely watchable performances from Antony Sher who makes Austin a frizzy-haired rodent nibbling timidly at the edges of life and from Bob Hoskins as the tattooed, teak-stained Lee who treats every inanimate object as if it were a personal enemy. Patricia Hayes also potters in amusingly as a horrified mom back from Alaska. But the play to me suggests a good writer flying on automatic pilot rather than taking a trip into the unknown.

From: *The Guardian,* December 11, 1981.

to yearn [jɜːn] to have a strong, sad desire to do s.th. **more in Thoreau** (saying) more in sorrow than in anger (Henry David Thoreau 1817–1862, American author and naturalist. His work "Walden, or Life in the Woods" stimulated the back-to-nature movement) **steeped** completely full of **to disintegrate** to break up into small pieces **to prove a point** *G.* etwas beweisen **to junk s.th.** ● *G.* etwas los werden **junked writer** ● *G.* abservierter Autor **to bash up** ● to destroy, break **recklessness** *G.* Tollkühnheit **vintage** best quality **thesis** *here:* opinion **to go awry** [əˈraɪ] *G.* schiefgehen **layer** *G.* Schicht **frizzy-haired** very curly like wool **rodent** [ˈrəʊdnt] *G.* Nagetier **to nibble** to eat with very small bites **teak** *G.* Teakholz **stained** the colour of **to potter** to walk around slowly with no real reason for doing so

Jochen Schmidt

Kain und Abel in Südkalifornien

„Goldener Westen" ist ein handfest und effektsicher gebautes kleines Schauspiel. Sam Shepard, der seit 1964 fast drei Dutzend Stücke geschrieben hat, hat den psychologischen Naturalismus wiederentdeckt. Er wandelt ungeniert in den Spuren von Ibsen und O'Neill, dessen Familientragödien er, aufs Handliche verkleinert, im "Goldenen Westen" in die Gegenwart weiterspinnt. Die große Geschichte der feindlichen Brüder, in einer Umwelt, die ihren Traum von der unendlichen Weite und der absoluten Freiheit demontiert und durch die blasse Vorstellung von der „sauberen" Wüste ersetzt hat: nie war sie so kleinmütig wie heute. In Düsseldorf hat Stefan Mayer für Shepards Stück eine Bühne gebaut, die den Ausschnitt aus der kalifornischen Realität wie ein Filmbild erscheinen läßt: ein zunächst beinahe leerer, verwinkelter Raum mit einem schmalen Fenster, durch dessen Blendläden die Außenwelt mehr zu ahnen als zu sehen ist. Die Inszenierung des 27 Jahre alten Amerikaners James Lyons, der bislang in Düsseldorf als Regieassistent gearbeitet hat, vermittelt mit vielen typischen Details einen Hauch von amerikanischer Westküstenatmosphäre. Sie ist sympathisch unprätentiös und handfest wie das Stück. Es könnte Karriere machen durch seine zentralen Rollen, die in Düsseldorf Berndt Hahn und Dieter Prochnow mit Leben füllen, ohne sie ins Mythische aufzublasen: Prochnow mit einer schäbigen, ranzigen Männlichkeit; Hahn mit einer Pseudointellektualität, deren Schwäche jederzeit in Gemeinheit umschlagen kann.

Excerpt from: *Frankfurter Allgemeine Zeitung*, 7.12.1982.

James Lyons

True West on the German stage

Düsseldorf, 21 January 1983

In bringing *True West* onto the German stage the major change we undertook was in the stage design. Instead of the naturalistic setting Shepard prescribes we constructed a much more abstract space, which at the beginning of the play is almost completely empty. We sought here to get at the essence of Shepard's world by placing the action in an at once neutral and unfamiliar atmosphere, thus avoiding false milieu associations and underlining a major theme in the

sought *here:* try (seek, sought, sought) **essence** the inner nature of s.th. **unfamiliar** not well known **to avoid** *G.* vermeiden **to underline** [ˌʌndəˈlaɪn] *G.* unterstreichen

play itself—the alienation of western man from his surroundings. The forces acting upon Austin and Lee—the threats of their identities, in a sense—converge on them from without, or "out there": the coyotes, the father, the producer, even the mother exist as determinants of their reality, determinants to which they have no real contact, over which they have no real control. We attempted to intensify the sensation of powerlessness in the face of these forces by initially placing all "objects" out of sight and then allowing them to appear and "take over" so to speak, as both characters slide further away from themselves and into a kind of (inner and outer) chaos.

Shepard differs from his American contemporaries in his ability to write metaphors for the stage. Though unmistakably American in outlook and language, Shepard's true obsession is reality itself. This places him closer to authors such as Beckett and Pinter than O'Neill or Miller—and makes him much more approachable for a European audience. *True West*, though primarily a comedy, and Shepard's "best-made" play, contains all the elements of his earlier, more surrealistic works. Characters are suddenly thrown into extreme situations that get out of their control; reality loses its moorings and drifts toward chaos. Austin describes at one point for instance his desperation when he discovers himself on streets "that turn out to be replicas of streets I remember. Streets I misremember. Streets I can't tell if I lived on or saw in a postcard" (50). Shepard is not a moralizer. He doesn't stand above the action, or attempt to formulate a "message" for his audience. Rather, he paints his figures from the inside out, which gives dimension to both their most existential and most banal tendencies. This intimacy and openness for the extreme lends Shepard's plays their wild humor and unflinching horror—and forbids anything approaching tragedy. Shepard's vision gives us at times a devastatingly nihilistic view of the American culture, but because Shepard himself never denies that he is a part of that culture we are allowed glimpses into the violent regions of the American mentality that other authors avoid, or don't know.

From: Albert-Reiner Glaap, "America's New West-Dreamscape and Reality".
In: Bredella, Lothar (ed.): *Die USA in Unterricht und Forschung*, Bochum 1984, p. 207.

alienation [ˌeɪlɪəˈneɪʃn] *G.* Befremdung **threat** *G.* Drohung **to converge** [kənˈvɜːdʒ] move towards and meet at one point **determinants** deciding factors **initially** at the beginning **to slide** to move slowly as on ice **outlook** person's way of seeing and understanding things **obsession** *G.* fixe Idee, Besessenheit **moorings** *G.* Verankerung **to drift** *G.* treiben **for instance** for example **desperation** *G.* Verzweiflung **to misremember** (poetic) remember incorrectly **tendencies** characteristics **unflinching** resolute **to devastate** [ˈdevəsteɪt] to ruin completely **to deny** to say s.th. is not true **to glimpse** get a quick, imperfect view of s.th.

2. Sam Shepard

An interview with Sam Shepard

Sam Shepard has been called the greatest American playwright of his generation, which was profoundly affected by the upheavals of the 1960s and came to professional maturity in the 1970s. His 40-some plays show elements of his background: the rhythms and attitudes of rock music, use of popular culture icons like cars and kitchen appliances, and a fascination with the myth of the American West as a place of opportunity and rootlessness.

Shepard's first plays were produced in 1964 in small avant-garde theaters in New York. Many of his works from this period reflect the creative ferment which was then taking place in art and music as well as experimental theater. After a three-year interlude in England in the early 1970s, he returned to the United States. He settled not in New York, but in rural California, and became playwright in residence at the Magic Theatre in San Francisco, where several of his major works, including Curse of the Starving Class, Buried Child, True West *and* Fool for Love, *were first produced.*

The following interview with Shepard was conducted by Amy Lippman, who was at the time a student at Harvard University.

What ties do you feel to the American West?

Well, it's all subjective, I just feel like the West is much more ancient than the East. Much more. It is. I don't know if you've traveled out West at all but there are areas like Wyoming, Texas, Montana and places like that, where you really feel this ancient thing about the land. Ancient. That it's primordial. Of course, you can say that about New England. But it doesn't have the same power to me, because it's this thing about space. No wonder these mysterious cults in Indian religions sprang up, you know? It wasn't as though these people were just ... just fell down from the sky. It has to do with the relationship between the land and the people—between the human being and the ground. I think that's typically western and much more attractive than this tight little forest civilization that happened back East. It's much more physical and emotional to me. New England and the East Coast have always been an intellectual community. Also, I was raised out West, so I guess it's just an outcome of my background. I just feel like I'll never get over the fact of being from the West.

From: *Dialogue* 4 (1985), pp. 50, 58f.

profound [prə'faʊnd] deep **to affect** to influence **upheaval** great and sudden change **maturity** state of being grown and fully developed **40-some** about 40 **root** *G.* Wurzel **ferment** ['fɜːment] state of social, political, artisitic unrest, change and excitement **interlude** interval **rural** of the countryside **curse** *G.* Fluch **to starve** to suffer or die from hunger **ties** feelings which hold people together e.g. friendship **ancient** extremely old **primordial** [praɪ'mɔːdjəl] existing from the beginning of time **tight** *G.* fest geschnürt, engherzig **to be raised** to grow up

3. Cain and Abel

Genesis 4

And the man had connection with Eve his wife, and she became with child and gave birth to Cain, and said, I have got a man from the Lord.

2 Then again she became with child and gave birth to Abel, his brother. And Abel was a keeper of sheep, but Cain was a farmer.

3 And after a time, Cain gave to the Lord an offering of the fruits of the earth.

4 And Abel gave an offering of the young lambs of his flock and of their fat. And the Lord was pleased with Abel's offering;

5 But in Cain and his offering he had no pleasure. And Cain was angry and his face became sad.

6 And the Lord said to Cain, Why are you angry? and why is your face sad?

7 If you do well, will you not have honour? and if you do wrong, sin is waiting at the door, desiring to have you, but do not let it be your master.

8 And Cain said to his brother, Let us go into the field: and when they were in the field, Cain made an attack on his brother Abel and put him to death.

9 And the Lord said to Cain, Where is your brother Abel? And he said, I have no idea: am I my brother's keeper?

10 And he said, What have you done? the voice of your brother's blood is crying to me from the earth.

11 And now you are cursed from the earth, whose mouth is open to take your brother's blood from your hand;

12 No longer will the earth give you her fruit as the reward of your work; you will be a wanderer in flight over the earth.

13 And Cain said, My punishment is greater than my strength.

14 You have sent me out this day from the face of the earth and from before your face; I will be a wanderer in flight over the earth, and whoever sees me will put me to death.

15 And the Lord said, Truly, if Cain is put to death, seven lives will be taken for his. And the Lord put a mark on Cain so that no one might put him to death.

16 And Cain went away from before the face of the Lord, and made his living-place in the land of Nod on the east of Eden.

From: *The Bible in Basic English.* Cambridge 1956, p. 13.

keeper of sheep shepherd **offering** *G.* Opfergabe **fruits of the earth** *(archaic)* harvest products **flock** large group of sheep **fat** *(archaic)* meat **honour** *G.* Ehre, Achtung **sin** *G.* Sünde **to desire** to wish for s.th. **keeper** *G.* Hüter **to curse** *G.* verfluchen **reward** [rɪ'wɔːd] *G.* Belohnung **flight** *G.* Flucht **punishment** *G.* Strafe **strength** *G.* Kraft **mark** *G.* Zeichen

4. Jacob and Esau

Genesis 25

21 Isaac made prayer to the Lord for his wife because she had no children; and the Lord gave ear to his prayer, and Rebekah became with child.

22 And the children were fighting together inside her, and she said, If it is to be so, why am I like this? So she went to put her question to the Lord.

23 And the Lord said to her, Two nations are in your body, and two peoples will come to birth from you: the one will be stronger than the other, and the older will be the servant of the younger.

24 And when the time came for her to give birth, there were two children in her body.

25 And the first came out red from head to foot like a robe of hair, and they gave him the name of Esau.

26 And after him, his brother came out, gripping Esau's foot; and he was named Jacob: Isaak was sixty years old when she gave birth to them.

27 And the boys came to full growth; and Esau became a man of the open country, an expert bowman; but Jacob was a quiet man, living in tents.

28 Now Isaac's love was for Esau, because Esau's meat was greatly to his taste: but Rebekah had more love for Jacob.

From: *The Bible in Basic English.* Cambridge 1956, p. 28.

prayer [preə(r)] *G.* Gebet **to give an ear to** *(archaic)* to listen to **servant** *G.* Diener **robe** *G.* Umhang **to grip** to hold very tightly **to come to full growth** *(archaic)* to grow up, become adult **bowman** ['bəʊmən] *G.* Bogenschütze **tent** *G.* Zelt

5. Mom and Mother

All my sons

ANN: (*Delicately.*) You mean am I still waiting for him?

MOTHER: Well, no, I don't expect you to wait for him but—

ANN: (*Kindly.*) But that's what you mean, isn't it?

MOTHER: Well ... yes.

ANN: Well, I'm not, Kate

MOTHER: (*Faintly.*) You're not?

ANN: Isn't it ridiculous? You don't really imagine he's—?

MOTHER: I know, dear, but don't say it's ridiculous, because the papers were full of it; I don't know about New York, but there was half a page about a man missing even longer than Larry, and he turned up from Burma.

CHRIS: (*Coming to* ANN.) He couldn't have wanted to come home very badly, Mom.

MOTHER: Don't be so smart.

CHRIS: You can have a helluva time in Burma.

ANN: (*Rises and swings around in back of* CHRIS.) So I've heard.

CHRIS: Mother, I'll bet you money that you're the only woman in the country who after three years is still—

MOTHER: You're sure?

CHRIS: Yes, I am.

MOTHER: Well, if you're sure then you're sure. (*She turns her head away an instant.*) They don't say it on the radio but I'm sure that in the dark at night they're still waiting for their sons.

CHRIS: Mother, you're absolutely.

MOTHER: (*Waving him off.*) Don't be so damned smart! Now stop it! (*Slight pause.*) There are just a few things you *don't* know. All of you. And I'll tell you one of them, Annie. Deep, deep in your heart you've always been waiting for him.

ANN: (*Resolutely.*) No, Kate.

MOTHER: (*With increasing demand.*) But deep in your heart, Annie!

CHRIS: She ought to know, shouldn't she?

MOTHER: Don't let them tell you what to think. Listen to your heart. Only your heart.

ANN: Why does your heart tell you he's alive?

MOTHER: Because he has to be.

ANN: But why, Kate?

MOTHER: (*Going to her.*) Because certain things have to be, and certain things can never be. Like the sun has to rise, it has to be. That's why there's God. Otherwise anything could happen. But there's God, so certain things can never happen. I would know, Annie—just like I knew the day he—(*Indicates* CHRIS.)—went into that terrible battle. Did he write me? Was it in the papers? No, but that morning I couldn't raise my head off the pillow. Ask Joe. Suddenly, I knew. I knew! And he was nearly killed that day. Ann, you *know* I'm right!

(ANN *stands there in silence, then turns trembling, going upstage.*)

ANN: No, Kate.

MOTHER: I have to have some tea. (FRANK *appears, carrying ladder.*)

From: Arthur Miller: "All My Sons". In: *Arthur Miller's Collected Plays.* New York 1967, pp. 77–78.

to imagine to think, believe **ridiculous** [rɪˈdɪkjʊləs] *G.* lächerlich **to be missing** not able to be found **to turn up** to arrive (unexpectedly) **smart** clever **to bet** *G.* wetten **instant** very short time **to wave s.o. off** *G.* abweisen **to indicate** to point to **pillow** *G.* Kopfkissen **ladder** *G.* Leiter

6. The Fading American Dream

Millions learning to cope with downward mobility

For millions of wage earners, the American dream is becoming the impossible dream. The unquestioning expectation of earning more money than one's parents did has died among many Amercians who were born during the baby boom years after World War II. Even the most basic tenet of the dream, that a young family will be more prosperous in its middle age, has grown more elusive. In fact, Americans now are struggling to fight off downward mobility at the end of a century that has stressed upward mobility.

The statistics tell the harsh story: Americans now must work hard just to stay in place economically.

Among the statistics:

● Average hourly earnings, adjusted for inflation, boomed in the 1950s and 1960s, but fell in the 1970s and showed no real growth in the first half of the 1980s.

● Average weekly earnings, held down slightly by a shorter work week, have declined by 14.3 percent since 1973, after accounting for inflation.

● Median household income, which was $ 26,433 in 1984, has dipped about 6 percent since 1973.

"From the end of World War II to 1973, everybody was getting better off, but from 1973 through now that has stopped", said Frank S. Levy, a professor of public policy at the University of Maryland.

Moonlighting, or working at extra jobs, is widespread. More married women with young children are working than ever before.

With their incomes failing to keep pace with their desires, Americans are increasingly using credit cards despite the persistently high interest rates.

Their money problems continue to mount. Business, reeling from toughening competition abroad, is keeping a tight rein on wages and on hiring.

Even the tax bills adopted by the House and Senate do not look like they will give the average American family much relief. Under either house's version, families with the median household income of $ 26,433 would receive tax cuts of only $ 200 or so.

Economists generally agree that the only way workers can manage to make substantial strides in real earnings during the years ahead is through steady and strong growth of productivity. But few economists are predicting that growth.

In the short run, this means that unless consumers continue piling up debt to fuel the economy, the nation's economic growth might slow during the rest of 1986 below the predicted 3 percent growth rate, and perhaps even below 2 percent.

In the longer run, a failure to grow could profoundly transform the American standard of living and the nation's economy.

Many economists point out that other countries such as Japan and West Germany have achieved higher growth in productivity. Some even suggest that the United States may be starting to undergo the same economic decline that the British have experienced in recent decades. (ENGL.)—NEW YORK TIMES

From: *World and Press*, 2.8.1986, Bremen (Eilers & Schünemann), p. 2.

downward mobility *G.* sozialer Abstieg **upward mobility** *G.* sozialer Aufstieg **wage earner** *G.* Lohnempfänger **tenet** ['ti:net] principle, maxim **prosperous** successful (financially) **elusive** [ɪ'lu:sɪv] difficult to reach **to struggle** to try hard to win against difficulties **to fight off** *G.* ankämpfen gegen, abwenden **to stress** to underline **harsh** disagreeable **to adjust** to arrange, put in order **to boom** to rise rapidly **median** ['mi:djən] middle, average **to dip** to fall **moonlighting** having an unofficial, additional job in your spare time **to fail to keep pace** *G.* nicht Schritt halten mit **increasingly** more and more **persistently** constantly **to mount** to go up, to increase **interest rate** *G.* Zinssatz **to reel** *G.* ins Wanken geraten **to keep a tight rein on s.th.** to allow little freedom **reins** *G.* Zügel **bill** law **relief** help **substantial** large **strides** steps (towards improvement) **to predict** to say what is likely to happen in the future **run** *here:* length of time **to pile up debts** *G.* Schulden anhäufen **to fuel** to give energy to s.th. **to achieve** to win, reach **to undergo** to experience

"I had no idea John Wayne was so big."

"They were filming a big western (what else?) the day we went to 'Old Tucson,' the movie location. I was telling Shirley how those cowboy hats and high-heel boots would make *anybody* look tall. Then we saw John Wayne. *Without* his hat. At least nine feet tall. *Sitting down.* I changed the subject."

YOU'LL SAVE MONEY AND HAVE MORE FUN-FILLED HOURS VISITING THE WEST BY USING OUR TIME SAVING ROUTING

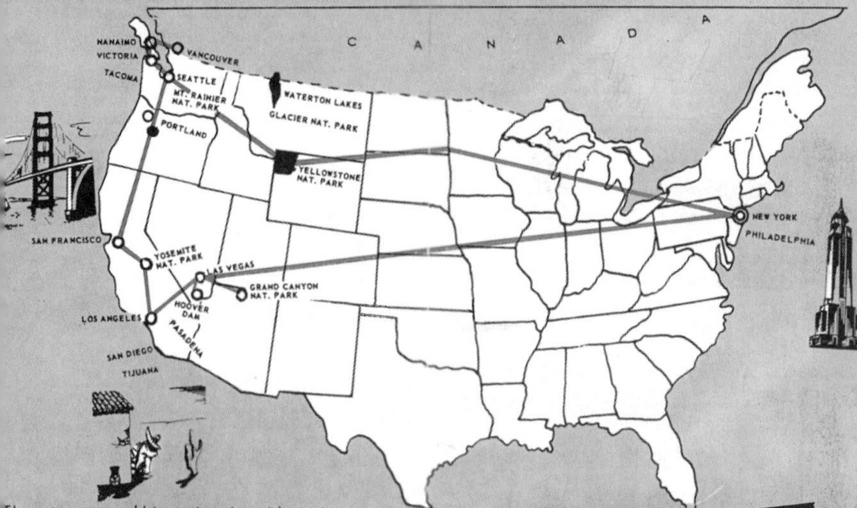

These tours are sold in conjunction with services of all approved IATA and ATC member carriers.

COME TO THE GOLDEN WEST!

That colorful exciting, vast section of the United States which means many things to many people. Some refer to it as VACATION PARADISE, which indeed it is. For here are scenic beauties unparalleled, vacation opportunities unsurpassed.

You have probably dreamed about a trip through the WEST, but never felt you had the time or money to see all the things you really wanted to see … or do all the things you wanted to do … why wait any longer? … this is the year of JETS … the promise fulfilled and then some. You can be in California in just a few hours … the most amazingly relaxing hours in anyone's travel experience. Flying high above the weather at near sonic speeds, your jet-liner is vibration-free, you will have the feeling of being suspended motionless in space as the vast panorama of the United States unfolds beneath you. Each western trip described in this folder encompasses the major points of interest you will want so see in each area visited. You can however, arrange for extra time at any of the cities on your itinerary. Your travel is completely independent so your days can be spent as you please. There are definite times for you to take advantage of local sights in many of the places you will be visiting (your personal travel itinerary will point these out to you).

You will find described in this folder several suggested itineraries for your projected Western Visit … select the one that fits your time allowance, your budget, your travel desires and start planning now!

See enclosed rate sheet for prices and hotels included.

Family Fun Park Where

The Wild West Lives Again!

The moment you enter Old Tucson, you've taken a step back in time and memory. You'll feel as though you've walked these streets before because this 320 acre settlement is the home of hundreds of major motion pictures, television shows and commercials. It all began in 1939 when Columbia Pictures created Old Tucson for the movie classic, "Arizona." Since then, the town has grown considerably. It now boasts its own Sound Stages as well as a complete family fun park. No longer reserved exclusively for Westerns, Old Tucson is also the setting for numerous modern day movies and television series. Frequently, two production companies will be working here at the same time, and when a show is in the making, visitors are welcome. Stuntmen-actors stage gun fights daily. Stagecoach and train rides provide a magnificent view of the territory. There's always something to see and do in this, the Southwest's most famous town.

TOUR 11 - OLD TUCSON AND DESERT MUSEUM

A few moments from busy downtown TUCSON, the visitor enters Gates Pass in the Tucson Mountains and gently descends to the valley floor where mighty saguaros stand as sentinels in the West Saguaro National Monument and to world-famous "OLD TUCSON," the reel-life setting of the pioneer West where the FUNtier begins. You've seen it on your movie or TV screen many times... most notably as a site for NBC's "HIGH CHAPARRAL." Reminiscent of yesteryear— Beware! lest you be caught in the midst of the daily gunfights in this replica of Tucson of 1870. From OLD TUCSON it's a short trip to one of the world's great efforts to display living animals, birds and plants of the Sonoran Desert in their natural setting, the internationally acclaimed ARIZONA-SONORA DESERT MUSEUM. The great Sonoran Desert region with its mountains and deserts offer a startling number and variety of animals and plants all introduced uniquely to the fortunate visitor strolling the Museum's many paths. Cameras are a must.

7. Paradox and Dream

Americans seem to live and breathe and function by paradox, but in nothing are we so paradoxical as in our passionate belief in our own myths. We truly believe ourselves to be natural-born mechanics and do-it-yourself-ers. We spend our lives in motor cars, yet most of us—a great many of us at least—do not know enough about a car to look in the gas tank when the motor fails. Our lives as we live them would not function without electricity, but it is a rare man or woman who, when the power goes off, knows how to look for a burned-out fuse and replace it. We believe implicitly that we are the heirs of the pioneers; that we have inherited self-sufficiency and the ability to take care of ourselves, particularly in relation to nature. There isn't a man among us in ten thousand who knows how to butcher a cow or a pig and cut it up for eating, let alone a wild animal. By natural endowment, we are great rifle shots and great hunters—but when hunting season opens there is a slaughter of farm animals and humans by men and women who couldn't hit a real target if they could see it. Americans treasure the knowledge that they live close to nature, but fewer and fewer farmers feed more and more people; and as soon as we can afford to we eat out of cans, buy frozen T.V. dinners, and jaunt the delicatessens. Affluence means moving to the suburb, but the American suburbanite sees, if anything, less of the country than the city apartment dweller with his window boxes and his African violets carefully tended under lights. In no country are more seeds and plants and equipment purchased, and less vegetables and flowers raised. [...]

The inventiveness once necessary for survival may also be a part of the national dream. Who among us has not bought for a song an ancient junked car, and with parts from other junked cars put together something that would run? This is not lost; American kids are still doing it. The dreams of a people either create folk literature or find their way into it; and folk literature, again, is always based on something that happened. Our most persistent folk tales—constantly retold in books, movies, and television shows—concern cowboys, gun-slinging sheriffs, and Indian fighters. These folk figures existed—perhaps not quite as they are recalled nor in the numbers indicated, but they did exist; and this dream also persists. Even businessmen in Texas wear the high-heeled boots and big hats, though they ride in air-conditioned Cadillacs and have forgotten the reason for the high heels. All our children play cowboy and Indian; the brave and honest sheriff who with courage and a six-gun brings law and order and civic virtue to a Western community is perhaps our most familiar hero, no doubt descended from the brave mailed knight of chivalry who battled and overcame evil with lance and sword. Even the recognition signals are the same; white hat, white armor—black hat, black shield. And in these moral tales, so deepset in us, virtue does not arise out of reason or orderly process of law—it is imposed and maintained by violence. [...]

For Americans too the wide and general dream has a name. It is called "the Amercian Way of Life". No one can define it or point to any one person or group who lives it, but it is very real nevertheless, perhaps more real than that equally remote dream the Russians call Communism. These dreams describe our vague yearnings toward what we wish we were and hope we may be: wise, just, compassionate, and noble. The fact that we have this dream at all is perhaps an indication of its possibility.

From: John Steinbeck, "America and Americans". In: *The American Dream.* Advanced Readings in English. (ed. G. Hocmard/M. Sommers/K. A. Sheram/H. Wolff). New York 1982, pp. 6–7.

to fail *here:* break down **rare** not often found **power** electricity **fuse** [fju:z] *G.* Sicherung **implicitly** [ɪm'plɪsɪtlɪ] completely, unquestioningly **heir** [eə(r)] *G.* Erbe/in **self-sufficiency** [selfsə'fɪʃnsɪ] not needing the help of others **ability** *G.* Fähigkeit **to butcher** to kill an animal for meat **let alone** *G.* geschweige (denn) **endowment** [ɪn'daʊmənt] *G.* Begabung **rifle** *G.* Gewehr **slaughter** to kill an animal (usually not to be eaten) **target** *G.* Zielscheibe **to treasure** *G.* (hoch)schätzen, hegen **to afford** *G.* sich etwas leisten **to jaunt** [dʒɔ:nt] *G.* sich schnell aufmachen (*hier:* in ein Delikatessengeschäft) **affluence** ['æflʊəns] *G.* Wohlstand **to dwell** to live **to tend s.th.** to look after s.th. lovingly **inventiveness** *G.* Erfindungsgabe **for a song** for almost nothing **junked** *G.* weggeworfen, ausrangiert **persistent** *G.* beharrlich, hartnäckig **to recall** to remember **to indicate** *here:* suggest **to persist** *G.* andauern **civic** of a city or town **mail** *G.* Panzerhemd **knight** *G.* Ritter **chivalry** ['ʃɪvlrɪ] *G.* Rittertum **deepset** deep-rooted **impose** *G.* auferlegen **remote** [rɪ'məʊt] very far away and difficult to reach **just** fair to others

[kaɪjot] ✓
[kaɪjotɪ]

987 6